D0395068

Praise

Praise for *Lost & Found*

"Lost & Found is a refreshingly honest story of grace, forgiveness, redemption and love. It is a must-read for anyone whose life has been impacted by an eating disorder, as well as for anyone who is a mother or a daughter!"
—Joani Jack, M.D., and Judy Halliday, R.N., authors of *Raising Fit Kids in a Fat World*

"With heartfelt writing and vivid scenes, Kathryn Slattery shows how the past can be redeemed in a bold and joyful present."
—Rick Hamlin, author of *Reading Between the Lines*

"This is the best book I have read about overcoming an eating disorder, and about experiencing healing, forgiveness and reconciliation through the power of God's love."
—Dr. William P. Wilson, Professor Emeritus of Psychiatry and founder of the program for Christianity in Medicine, Duke University, Durham, North Carolina

"With immense courage, Kathryn Slattery has walked back into the dark places in her own life, emerging with life-transforming insights."
—Elizabeth Sherrill, author of *All the Way to Heaven* and *The Hiding Place*

"Lost & Found takes us on a journey across the complicated terrain of one woman's heartbreaking but ultimately redemptive relationship with her mother. This is a worthy read for anyone on the quest to find meaning and hope from the brokenness of their past."
—Ian Morgan Cron, author of *Chasing Francis: A Pilgrim's Tale*

"An intimate and honest portrayal of a daughter's struggle to love her mother as she learns to love herself. . . . This memoir is an inspiration for all who are looking for hope and healing."
—Daniel C. Walker, Executive Director, Fellowship of Christians in Universities and Schools (FOCUS)

"Lost & Found is the moving account of a daughter's journey to wholeness. Kathryn Slattery explores in depth a complex mother/daughter relationship and in the process helps the reader discover truths that are relevant and applicable to every relationship."
—James N. Lane, Founder, New Canaan Society

LOST & FOUND

ONE DAUGHTER'S STORY
of AMAZING GRACE

Kathryn Slattery

Guideposts.
New York, New York

Lost & Found

ISBN-13: 978-0-8249-4734-7

Published by Guideposts
16 East 34th Street
New York, New York 10016

Distributed by Ideals Publications, a Guideposts company
535 Metroplex Drive, Suite 250
Nashville, Tennessee 37211

Guideposts and *Ideals* are registered trademarks of Guideposts.

ACKNOWLEDGMENTS
Every attempt has been made to credit the sources of copyrighted material used in this
book. If any such acknowledgment has been inadvertently omitted or misattributed,
receipt of such information would be appreciated.

Jacket and interior design by Marisa Jackson
Jacket photo © Catherine Ledner/Getty Images

Printed and bound in the United States of America

For my mother.

Acknowledgments

This book is written with heartfelt gratitude to Marilyn Moore, my editor at Guideposts, to Mark Sweeney, my agent, and to so many loving friends and family—especially my sister, my children Katy and Brinck, and my dear husband Tom. Your generous encouragement and prayers along the way have meant more to me than words can ever say.

Dear Reader,

As M. Scott Peck famously wrote in the first line of *The Road Less Traveled*, "Life is difficult." At the same time, I truly believe that in God's economy, nothing in life goes to waste—that something beautiful and good can come out of life's most difficult and challenging circumstances and mistakes. This is the miracle of God's redemptive grace.

All of us have a story to tell. When we choose to share our stories, extraordinary things can happen. We are able to laugh at ourselves. We realize we are not alone with our various human frailties, fears and failures. Our hearts mysteriously expand, and we experience an increased capacity to forgive and love—not only others, but ourselves. We appreciate, in a new way, how much we *need* each other. It is my heartfelt hope and prayer that this story will not only serve to engage and entertain you, but through God's grace, might also serve as a source of encouragement, healing and hope.

Finally, in order to most truthfully tell this story, the names of some characters have been changed.

With blessings always,

Kathryn Slattery

www.KathrynSlattery.com

Contents

Amazing grace! (how sweet the sound)
That sav'd a wretch like me!
I once was lost, but now am found,
Was blind, but now I see.

—*John Newton (1725–1807)*

My Name Is Kathryn . . .

BUT EVERYONE CALLS ME KITTY. When I was growing up, the only person who called me Kathryn was my mother, and then only when I was in really big trouble. Like the afternoon when I was three, and a photographer came to the house to take our family portrait, and I had a big old rip-roaring temper tantrum that ruined the whole day and sent the photographer packing. "Kathryn Louise Brinckerhoff!" my mother scolded, as the photographer pulled out of the driveway in a cloud of dust. "You should be *ashamed* of yourself!" I was. Or the time when I was six, and we visited my grandparents, and I accidentally left the iron on and burned a stinky, black iron-shaped scorch mark on the laundry room's speckled linoleum floor. Even my beloved grandmother yelled at me that day. Then she turned to my mother. "Bessie!" she scolded, "You'd better watch out, or you're going to spoil this child rotten." I could see the hurt expression in my mom's eyes, and I remember thinking that her mother's approval must have been very important to her too.

For a long time I assumed I got my nickname from my

parents. But it turned out it was my big sister Carolyn who thought it up, back when I was a baby. Carolyn said that when I slept, I curled up in the corner of my crib like a small cat. My sister always liked cats. She still does. I'm actually more of a dog person. Maybe this is because my best, most loyal childhood friend was a fawn-colored boxer with white paws named Roxie. But don't get me wrong. Cats are okay too.

Some things in life chosen for us by others can be easily changed—names, for instance. In addition to Kitty, derivatives of Kathryn include Kathy, Katy, Kate, Kay, Kat and Kit. Over the years, I could have changed my name if I had wanted. As it turned out, I was happy with my sister's choice, although I did change the spelling. Initially, my mother and sister spelled my name "Kitti." They thought the "i" was more stylish and cute. But from the time I was five years old and learned how to write, I preferred the traditional old-fashioned spelling. "Kitty" was somehow more accurate and down-to-earth, like a *real* kitty cat. Or like Miss Kitty, the tough-talking redheaded saloon owner with the heart of gold on the popular TV western *Gunsmoke*. The funny thing was, even though I changed the spelling of my name, my mother and sister didn't. They kept on spelling it Kitti. Maybe they wanted me to be more stylish and cute.

For better or worse, there are many things in life chosen

for us by others that cannot so easily be changed. The particular details of our life circumstances, for instance. Our families' histories and backgrounds. Where we grow up. Moves, accidents, illnesses, divorces and deaths that happen along the way. Our genetic makeup. The way we're psychologically and emotionally wired. Our birth order. And, of course, those two mysterious people who at times—especially to a child—appear all-powerful and responsible for *everything*: our parents.

This is the story of my mother and me—two very different people. I did not choose my mother. And while she did choose to have me (a choice for which I am eternally grateful), I suspect there were many ways that I did not turn out to be exactly the daughter she might have hoped for. I know there were many times when she was not exactly the kind of mother I wanted and needed.

So what were my mother and I to do? No matter how hard we might try, we could not change each other. No one person ever can change another. This being the case, was it possible that we could ever accept each other? Appreciate each other? Know each other? Love each other?

Perhaps.

But it would take more than our mere human wills, individual or combined.

It would take a miracle.

Planet Miami

WHEN I WAS GROWING UP, my father's job caused us to move a lot. I was born in Niagara Falls, New York, my mother's home town, and when I was a baby we moved to Tampa, Florida. I was three when we moved to Charleston, South Carolina, and when I was five, we moved to Medfield, Massachusetts, a woodsy Boston suburb.

Then, when I was ten, we moved to Miami. The girls at Miami's Groveland Elementary School were a lot more grown-up than the friends I had left behind back in small-town Medfield. They didn't play with dolls. They didn't climb trees. Instead of rubber-toed lace-up Keds, they wore Thom McAn dress-up flats to school, *without* socks. Some of the girls had boyfriends. And shaved their legs. And wore bras. I was especially mystified as to how one day little blonde Katie McKeen was flat as a board and the next day looked like my Barbie.

"Falsies," said Billy Smith, who sat behind me in Mr. Sanders' sixth grade class. "She lifted 'em."

Billy looked a little bit like Elvis, and a little bit like

James Dean. He wore his dark curly hair slicked back with Brylcreem, black jeans and a white T-shirt with the sleeves rolled up. It was easy to imagine that the pencil tucked behind his ear was a cigarette.

I stared at him, uncomprehending.

"Falsies," he repeated. "Fake boobs. Katie shoplifted them."

Fake boobs? Shoplifted? The words were English, but Billy might as well have been speaking Chinese.

Katie McKeen, with her flirty southern accent and chipped front tooth, was the most popular girl at Groveland Elementary. She was also a favorite of Mr. Sanders, who frequently summoned her to sit on his lap. Another one of Mr. Sanders' class pets was Geena Barrows, who wore pearly pink nail polish and strawberry flavored Bonne Bell lip gloss. She spent a lot of time on his lap too.

Marvin Sanders was my first male teacher. A bachelor, he wore his dark oily hair parted to one side, and his half-lens reading glasses so low on his nose they looked like they might slip off any second. The teachers at my old elementary school in Medfield had rewarded students by inviting them to stay after class to wipe the blackboard, or empty the trash basket, or take erasers outside to clap them clean. While I very much wanted Mr. Sanders to like me, I wasn't so sure I wanted to sit on his lap.

ONE DAY THE ASSISTANT PRINCIPAL came to the classroom and one by one summoned members of our class to the principal's office to be interviewed by two policemen—actually a policeman and a police lady.

"Tell me," the lady officer asked, "Have you ever been touched in an inappropriate way by your teacher?"

"What do you mean?" I asked.

"Well, for example, has Mr. Sanders ever asked you to sit on his lap?"

"No," I said, biting my nail. "I—I don't think he likes me."

"Have you ever observed other girls sitting on his lap?"

"Yes," I said. "Katie McKeen. And Geena Barrows. And maybe some others, I guess."

"Thank you," the officer smiled. "You've been very helpful."

I was relieved the officer hadn't asked me about Katie's shoplifted falsies. But I returned to class feeling confused and guilty. Why were the police asking *me* questions? Had *I* done something wrong? Had telling the officer about Katie and Geena been the right thing to do? And other than being kind of weird, what was so wrong about sitting on a teacher's lap anyway? None of it made any sense. So I pushed it out of my mind.

One Monday morning I heard the kids talking about a big party at Geena's house that had taken place over the weekend. There had been drinking and kissing and—other things. I wasn't sure what "doing it" meant. When I turned around in my seat and asked Billy Smith, he rolled his eyes.

"Sheesh," he said. "You're hopeless."

A FEW DAYS LATER, the assistant principal appeared at our classroom door and motioned with his index finger for me to come forward.

"Your mother is in the office waiting for you," he said.

Uh-oh, I thought. *This can't be good.*

She stood inside the office door, slender and tall, arms crossed and tapping her foot nervously. Her toenails were perfectly manicured and painted a bright Revlon Fire and Ice red. She wore green cat's-eye sunglasses and a stylish straw hat. Auburn curls framed her pretty face, and her tiny waist was cinched in with a matching straw belt. My mother was naturally thin. "How I wish I could put on weight," she would sigh. "But no matter how hard I try, I just can't seem to gain."

Oh, to have such a problem.

Back in Medfield, I'd been an active, athletic kid. But since moving to Miami I'd started putting on weight. In Miami there were no woods to explore, no trees to climb. Plus, it was so darn hot. One day while playing tetherball under the blazing Florida sun, I thought I'd keel over from the heat. Back in Medfield, on summer days when it was hot,

I would go downstairs and play in our cool basement. But in Miami it was hot *all* the time. And our new house didn't have a basement. Although one girl in my class did have something *sort of* like a basement in her backyard. It was called a "bomb shelter." But it was sealed tightly shut with rusty metal bolts, and we were forbidden to play in it. *Why*, I wondered, *would anyone want a bomb shelter?* I thought the war was something that had ended a long, long time ago.

"Quickly," with a steely grip my mother steered me out the principal's door and toward the school parking lot. "Get in the car."

"What's going on?" I asked.

"Your father called from work, and he wants us to get out of Miami. Fast. I packed your suitcase. We'll drive north to Tampa, where Dad will meet us later tonight. He says we'll be safe there." She reached to turn the chrome-trimmed knob on the radio of our Ford Falcon station wagon, the kind with the fake wood paneling on the sides.

On the radio, President Kennedy addressed the nation in grave tones. Spy photos had revealed that Cuba had Soviet nuclear missiles pointed directly at us, and our military forces were on full alert.

Cuba, my mother explained, was less than one hundred miles off the coast of Florida.

So that's why houses in Miami have bomb shelters!

I pulled my dog Roxie close, and gazed out the window

as we turned west onto Alligator Alley, a flat stretch of high-way that cut through the Everglades to Florida's Gulf Coast. From there we would travel two hundred miles north to Dunedin, a sleepy seaside community near Tampa, where my mother's parents had a winter home.

At the Alligator Alley rest stop, native Seminole women sold handwoven baskets and primitive button-eyed dolls. Wearing long, colorful embroidered skirts, they regarded us with sad dark eyes. Back on the road, the pass-ing landscape was swampy, bleak and desolate, which matched my mood exactly. Two hours out of Miami, all there was to listen to was hillbilly music and preachers, so my mother turned off the radio.

We rode on in silence.

As I gazed into the distance where the endless flat stretch of gray asphalt met the sky, it occurred to me that now might be a good time to tell my mother about Mr. Sanders and all the strange goings-on at school. Maybe she would be able to help me make sense of it all.

So I summoned all my courage, sucked in my breath, and told her in one great exhaled blurt of words how none of the girls played with dolls anymore, and how some of them had boyfriends and shaved their legs and wore bras. I told her about Geena Barrows' wild parties. I told her how Mr. Sanders invited pretty girls to sit on his lap, but not me, and how I was worried he didn't like me. I almost told her about my meeting with the police—but at the last second, afraid I might get in trouble, I chickened out.

There was a pause as I waited anxiously for my mother's reaction, and for her answers.

Finally she spoke.

"Well!" she said brightly, "I think we should invite Mr. Sanders over for dinner. My goodness, he's your *teacher*. I'm sure he's a very nice man."

Didn't she hear a word I said?

We continued to drive on in silence.

"Isn't the Florida sky beautiful?" she suddenly asked. "So many colors. And such gorgeous clouds!"

I fixed my eyes on the green tinted band at the top of the windshield. The air around the car shimmered with waves of heat, and for a moment I felt as though I was trapped in a space capsule, traveling through the atmosphere of some strange, inhospitable, dangerous planet. Peering ahead, the heat played tricks on my eyes. At any given point in the distance, the pavement looked shiny and wet. But once we got there, the road was dry as dust.

I wrapped my arms around Roxie and closed my eyes. Feeling lost and alone, I tried not to think about school and Mr. Sanders and Cuba.

As it turned out, there was no missile attack, and after spending the weekend with my grandparents, the three of us returned to Miami safe and sound.

"Isn't it great to be home?" my mother asked, as we pulled into the driveway.

No, I thought. I missed my old house. And school. And friends.

THAT NIGHT I TRIED TO SLEEP, but the air-conditioning was broken and the buzz of the rotating electric fan kept waking me up. It was too hot for Roxie too. Instead of sleeping where she usually did at the foot of my rumpled bed, she was stretched out on the cool terrazzo floor.

I turned on my bedside lamp and reached for a new book called *A Wrinkle in Time* by a writer named Madeleine L'Engle. The story was about a girl named Meg who was searching for her lost father, and something called a *tesseract,* which allowed the characters to travel back and forth in time.

What I'd give to be able to travel back in time, I thought. *Back to Medfield and the way things used to be . . .*

On Top of the World

BEFORE MOVING TO MIAMI, I guess you could say I was a tomboy. Oh, I liked playing with dolls, all right. And dressing up in my big sister's tulle and taffeta prom dresses. And jumping on my rubber-tipped pogo stick until my brain felt like scrambled eggs. And roller skating. And hula-hooping.

But what I liked best was climbing trees . . .

HIGHER AND HIGHER I CLIMBED. Small branches and twigs snapped, releasing the sweet scent of pine. Sticky amber sap dripped on the white rubber toes of my new red Keds. No matter. Hand over hand I reached for the next tree limb, and the next, keeping my eyes focused on the brilliant blue sky above. Suddenly, there were no more branches to climb. There was just the sky and clouds and the scarlet flash of a cardinal's wings.

Clinging to the treetop, at once terrified and ecstatic, I swayed back and forth in the early autumn breeze. All around me murmuring pines, sturdy oaks, whispering elms and slender birches rustled and swayed and joined the dance.

Yes, back when I was eight years old, I was on top of the world.

From my treetop vantage point, Medfield, Massachusetts, in 1960 didn't look very different than when the town had been founded more than three hundred years earlier by Puritan settlers. Located eighteen miles southwest of Boston and steeped in Colonial history, Medfield was a picturesque hamlet of rolling woodland hills, rambling stone walls, sparkling creeks and ponds brimming with fat trout.

Waiting for me on the forest floor below, Roxie pricked her black pointy ears and barked. Drifting above the tree-tops, carried by the wind, we both recognized the distant trill of my mother's silver whistle calling us home. Reluctantly, I climbed down the tree and dropped from the lowest branch to the ground, landing with a thud on a soft blanket of yellow pine needles.

"C'mon, Roxie. Time to go."

Roxie wagged her little stump of a tail and nuzzled the back of my knee with her wet black nose. I scratched her behind the ear and reached down to pick up a glass mayonnaise jar with jagged air-holes punched in the tin lid. Pressing my nose against the glass, I inspected the contents: two glistening red-backed salamanders plucked earlier in the day from their hiding place beneath a crumbling log. They returned my gaze with beady unblinking eyes.

Scampering home along an old stone wall, the sharp point of an authentic hand-carved Wampanoag arrowhead stashed deep in my pants pocket pricked my thigh. I grimaced. Then grinned. *What a prize!* Quite unexpectedly, I'd discovered the old arrowhead while hunting for salamanders. In school I learned how back in the wee morning hours of February 21, 1676, during the height of the Indian Wars, Medfield had been burned to the ground by the fearsome Chief Metacomet, known as King Philip to the colonists. Seventeen townspeople had been killed. *Scalped!* I shuddered at the thought.

In the distance, the dense woods opened to reveal a clearing with a blueberry patch and our shady backyard. On Fairview Road, Medfield's newest subdivision, all the houses were pretty much alike: split-level, three bedrooms, one-car attached garage, some with finished basements. Each house had a big bay picture window. On the previous Christmas we had been the first family on the block to decorate ours with a shiny aluminum tree with a rotating color wheel. Many nights Roxie and I would sit side by side and watch, transfixed, as the glittering tree magically changed from red . . . to blue . . . to yellow . . . to green. Between red and blue the wheel squeaked, which caused Roxie's ears to perk and her brow to furrow just the tiniest bit.

What a great day, I thought, as I climbed the steps to

the screened-in back porch. *To think I found two salaman-ders and an honest-to-goodness Indian arrowhead!* I could hardly wait to show off my treasures.

Inside the house, I heard the growl of the vacuum cleaner.

"Hey, Mom!"

Intent on her task, she didn't hear me. Tall and slender, she wore a pastel pink shirtwaist dress, beige heels, pearl clip-on earrings, and yellow rubber gloves. Her posture was perfect as she pushed the noisy upright Hoover back and forth across the living room carpet. Hanging from a black silk cord around her neck, her silver whistle dangled back and forth hypnotically. An elegant auburn-haired beauty, sometimes my mother reminded me of the actress Katherine Hepburn. Other times, she reminded me of TV's then-reigning queen of comedy, Lucille Ball—more because of her red hair than her sense of humor.

"*Mom!*"

I thrust the mayonnaise jar with the two salamanders toward her, prompting her to recoil in disgust.

"*Ew-w-w!*" She wrinkled her nose.

I dug in my pocket for the arrowhead. "Look what else I found!" Extending my open palm, I offered her the dirt-encrusted arrowhead as though it were a precious jewel.

"Not now," she shook her head. "Go wash your hands. We've got company coming for dinner in less than an hour. It's their first time here, and I want everything to be perfect."

She said the last sentence more to herself than to me. Sometimes I wondered why my mother cared so much about what other people thought. Why it was so important to her that everything be "under control" and "perfect." Why she was so competitive. Even when she joined me for a casual game of pick-up-sticks or jacks on the kitchen floor, she never forgot that she was playing to *win*. That's when she was happiest. That's when her blue-green eyes sparkled most brightly and when she laughed most easily— a pretty, tinkly laugh that reminded me of ice cubes in a tall cool glass of tangy lemonade on a hot summer day.

Trying not to show my disappointment, I shoved the arrowhead back in my pocket and picked up the jar with the salamanders.

"Where's Dad?"

My mother tilted her head toward the family room.

Sitting in a wing-backed chair, the collar of his blue oxford-weave shirt unbuttoned and his tie loosened, my father was flipping through the pages of the latest issue of *Life* magazine while absentmindedly blowing a chain of perfectly cylindrical smoke rings.

"Hey there, Scooter!" He extinguished his Camel in an ashtray that was metal on top, and weighted on the bottom with a red-plaid beanbag. "Watcha got there in the jar?" He opened his arms wide.

"Salamanders!"

I jumped in his lap and flung my arms around his neck. My father was the only person who called me Scooter. Scooter McGee. Don't ask me why. But I liked it.

MY FATHER WORKED as New England's District Sales Manager for National Airlines. His office was located at Boston's Logan Airport. When people asked my mother what her husband did, she said that he was an *executive*. When she said the word, I could hear the pride in her voice. She also said that my dad was a *people person*. There was no doubt about it. He wasn't a clown, or loud, or anything like that. He was just fun and easy to be around. When he smiled, his pale blue eyes crinkled with kindness, and he always knew just what to say to put others at ease. With his thin moustache and air of sophistication, sometimes he reminded me of the movie star David Niven. Other times he reminded me of Jackie Gleason—especially when he rolled his eyes, clapped his hands inversely and intoned in a spot-on impersonation of the great TV comic, "And *awa-a-a-aay* we go!"

For as long as I could remember, I'd always felt closer to my father than to my mother. My mother and I were like two negatively polarized magnets—like the plastic apple and orange stuck on our refrigerator door—fighting against an invisible force that worked to push us apart. She was always so busy shopping and cleaning and making casseroles and hosting bridge parties. I don't know how she found the time to take me to Brownie meetings, piano and ballet lessons. Plus the Van Gogh exhibit at the Isabella Stewart Gardner Museum. And the Young People's Concert Series at the Boston Pops. You'd think with all those hours together in the car, we'd be better acquainted. But we weren't.

My father, on the other hand, was the listener, the nurturer, the parent who sought me out.

My father was *fun*.

Indeed the town was still buzzing about the previous Saturday when my father, an avid fly fisherman, had finally hooked the legendary monster rainbow trout that for years had eluded anglers from the depths of Miss Jewel's pond. Miss Jewel was the town spinster. Although the sign on her property clearly read "NO TRESPASSING," that didn't stop my father from donning his chest-high rubber waders, venturing onto the overgrown estate in the predawn darkness, and casting his line into the cool black water . . . *Bam!* The big fish bit. Hard. And for two days the twenty-two-inch, fourteen-pound glassy-eyed trout laid in honorific state on a bed of crushed ice in our kitchen sink, while neighbors stood in line to view the deceased and shake my father's hand. I was so *proud* of him.

On Saturday mornings, he took me fly fishing at Medfield's Rocky Woods Reservation, six square miles of unspoiled hiking and cross-country skiing paths wrapped around Chickering Pond, which was stocked with rainbow, brook and brown trout. Wrapping his strong arms around mine, he showed me how to grasp the fishing rod just so, and with a quick flick of the wrist, cast the line out long and easy—*slo-o-o-owly* reeling it in, teasing the fish along the way. He showed me how to carefully remove the hooks from the mouths of wriggling small fry and gently release them into the pond's shimmering green water. He showed me how to whack the keepers on the head with a stainless steel ice-cracker to put them out of their gasping-for-life misery. How to cut off their heads, and gut and fillet them too. On one father-daughter outing at Rocky Woods, we caught the most trout and won first prize: a case of Coca Cola! Back home, when I accidentally filleted my finger with a sharp fishing knife, my father was the one who washed the wound under cold running water and tenderly applied a Band-Aid. My mother always said my father could have been a doctor, he was so good in emergencies. I was glad she said "could have" instead of "should have," because "should have" would have implied that being an airlines executive wasn't as good as being a doctor, which might have hurt my father's feelings. And I didn't want my mother, or anyone else, to *ever* hurt my father's feelings.

NOW, I RESTED MY HEAD on his chest and listened to the reassuring resonance of his deep voice and the low rumble of his laughter. There was something about my father that made me feel so safe, accepted, and—well—loved.

The Bird Cake

THE SATURDAY MORNING had started off like any other in Medfield, with *Mighty Mouse* cartoons in the family room, and a TV tray with a steaming bowl of Maypo maple flavored hot cereal and a tall glass of milk sweetened with Bosco chocolate syrup. Then, while carrying my breakfast dishes to the sink, I asked my mother if I could bake a cake. I knew she loved to bake and I expected her to be delighted that her younger daughter was at last showing an interest in something other than climbing trees and catching salamanders.

"I'm sorry, Kitty," she said. "This really isn't a good time. I've got a million things to do today." She wiped her hands on her apron. "Why don't you ask your sister?"

Ten years older than I, Carolyn was a sophomore at the University of Massachusetts, two hours away by car in Amherst. Home from college for the weekend, she was still sound asleep. Not bothering to knock, I opened her door and jumped on her bed.

"Mom told me to ask you if you'll help me bake a cake! So will you?" I bounced impatiently. "*Please?*"

"Huh?" Carolyn pulled a pillow over her head. "Can't you see I'm sleeping?"

"But Mom *said*!"

"Oh, all right." Carolyn sat up on her elbows and yawned. "But give me a few minutes, okay?"

"Hooray!" I bounced off the bed onto the floor. "See you in the kitchen!"

On her senior page in the 1959 Medfield High School yearbook, the editors had described *Carolyn Anne Brinckerhoff* as "pretty to walk with and witty to talk with." It was something of a miracle that Carolyn was able to walk at all. At age fourteen, she had contracted polio, and for two and a half years she wore a cumbersome full-length brace on her left leg.

I was four years old when my sister got polio. We had recently moved from Tampa, Florida, to Charleston, South Carolina, and were living in a rental house on the shore of a backwater bayou. Initially, the doctor had misdiagnosed my sister's illness and told my parents that Carolyn just had "a cold in her leg." Everyone was very upset when it turned out she had polio.

One sultry summer evening, I was standing in the kitchen with my mother and sister when ominous black storm clouds gathered over the bayou. The wind picked up, and we heard the distant rumble of thunder. As the summer storm moved closer, brilliant flashes of lightning lit the sky, quickly followed by sharp cracks of thunder.

Outside, a family of tiny peeper frogs clung for dear life with their spatula-like toes to the screen of the open window above the kitchen sink. Suddenly, the air in the room became electric—the hair on my arms and neck prickled—and there was an earsplitting crack, like a gunshot. We all screamed and watched in wide-eyed horror as a fiery orange ball of lightning, about the size of a grapefruit, passed *through* the screen above the kitchen sink, landed on the counter, and then dropped to the floor, bouncing twice before vanishing with a loud, sizzling crackle.

Terrified, I ran screaming from the kitchen into the living room where I covered my eyes with my hands and curled up into a sobbing ball on the sofa.

Moments later, I felt a gentle touch on my head. I opened my eyes expecting to see my mother. But it was my sister who stood over me.

"It's okay," she said. "The lightning is gone. It's safe to go back in the kitchen."

She lifted me off the sofa and set me on the floor.

"C'mon," she said, wrapping her arm around my shoulder. "Let's go be with Mom. She's pretty shaken up."

Except for the sad fact that the family of peeper frogs had been fried to a blackened crisp, it would seem that my sister was right. Everything was okay. But now *two* bad, scary things had happened. Mom, Carolyn and I had nearly been killed, like the peeper frogs, by a freakish ball of lightning.

And my sister had polio.

Am I going to get polio too? I wondered. When I asked my sister this question, she reassured me that I would not. She said that there was something called a "polio vaccine" that had just come out, and that would protect me.

A few days later, I observed my mother peering through the crack of Carolyn's partially opened bedroom door. Sitting on the edge of her bed, she wore a white Peter Pan collared blouse, an aqua crinoline skirt and bobby socks. Lying on the floor was her brace, a grotesque contraption with leather straps and two metal bars bolted to a forlorn black and white saddle shoe. Standing silently behind my mother, quiet as a shadow, I watched as Carolyn opened the drawer on her bedside table, took out a yellow cloth tape measure and circled it around her pale, atrophied calf. When I looked up at my mother, her eyes were damp with tears. I didn't understand why. It seemed to me that Carolyn was the one who should have been crying.

BECAUSE OF OUR TEN-YEAR AGE DIFFERENCE, Carolyn was like a second mother to me when I was very young. Even now, she protectively gripped my hand when we crossed the street. Sometimes she let me listen to her collection of 45 rpm records—Paul Anka's "Diana," and Elvis Presley's "Hound Dog" and "Love Me Tender." I loved stacking the small black discs on the fat round spindle of her boxy portable record player with the pink plastic handle, and dancing like the teenagers on *American Bandstand*. Most fun were the novelty recordings . . . "Flying Purple People Eater," "Itsy Bitsy Teeny Weenie Yellow Polka Dot Bikini," "Witch Doctor," and Alvin and the Chipmunks' "Christmas Song."

At eight o'clock on Sunday nights the two of us curled up on the family room sofa with root beer floats and watched *The Ed Sullivan Show* together. Carolyn made me laugh with her funny imitation of Señor Wences, the ventriloquist who talked to a puppet in a box named Pedro— "S'okay? S'awright!"—and to Johnny, his lipstick-smeared hand.

Even though she had polio, Carolyn could still drive. When she rolled down the window of our mother's tomato-red Studebaker and invited me to hop in the back seat to go candlepin bowling with her teenage girlfriends, I felt like she really meant it—that I wasn't just the kid sister tagging along. In the summertime she took me swimming at Farm Pond, and on the way home treated me to frosty blueberry frappes at Bubbling Brook, the local ice-cream hangout.

Eventually Carolyn's brace came off, and by the time she was a senior in high school, you could hardly notice her limp. When she was named first runner-up in the Miss Medfield contest, my mother said the only reason she didn't win was because she wore a black dress, which made her look "too sophisticated." I thought for sure the contest had to have been rigged. With her shoulder-length strawberry blonde hair and our mother's pearl necklace, Carolyn was beautiful. Just like Miss America . . .

Now she stood next to me in the kitchen. She wore a crisp white shirt, black pedal pushers and matching black flats.

"So you want to bake a cake," Carolyn said, placing her hands on her hips and cocking her head. She put a finger to her mouth and pursed her lips. "Hmm-m-m. Since this is your first cake, let's start with something simple. How about a nice devil's food cake from a mix?"

I nodded eagerly.

I held out my arms and stood perfectly still while Carolyn tied a frilly red apron around my waist. I observed carefully as she showed me how to preheat the oven to 350 degrees . . . how to cut out circles of waxed paper to line the bottom of two aluminum baking pans . . . how to measure one cup of water, crack two eggs, and set the dial on the Hamilton Beach electric mixer to "Medium."

Finally, it was time to pour the velvety smooth batter into the baking pans waiting on the kitchen table. Carefully, I lifted the ceramic mixing bowl and began to carry it from the counter to the table. But the bowl was heavier than I thought. It slipped from my fingers and I watched in dismay as it fell—as though in slow motion—and landed with a sickening crash on the black and white checkered linoleum floor. Chocolate batter splattered everywhere, and the bowl cracked into pieces.

For a moment no one spoke. Tears welled up in my eyes, and I wondered if I was in trouble. I braced myself for a good scolding.

But Carolyn didn't yell.

"Don't worry," she said, just as brightly as when we had started baking. "We can make a bird cake."

"A bird cake?" I asked. "What's that?"

"We'll just scoop this mess up, broken bowl and all, pour it in a big pan and bake it," she said. "Then we'll put it out in the back yard for the birds. That way nothing goes to waste."

"And the birds will like it?" I asked.

"Even better," she said. "The birds will *love* it."

Later that afternoon, we watched from the back porch as a flock of purple finches swooped in from the woods to feast on the pile of broken crockery and chocolate cake.

"You see," said Carolyn, "how nothing goes to waste?"

I nodded.

I missed my sister when she went back to college.

A lot.

Sweet Dreams

WE'D JUST FINISHED DINNER when the doorbell rang. It was Karen Saffarian, my wiry, dark-haired friend who lived across the street. Karen's parents, Maggie and Mike, were Armenian. When I first met Karen, I worried that the reason she was so skinny was because she was one of the "poor starving Armenians" that we prayed for when we said grace at Thanksgiving. My father reassured me that she was not. Mrs. Saffarian worked weekends as a hostess at O'Malley's Steak House, and Karen was the first girl on Fairview Road to get a Barbie doll. My mother disapproved. She thought I was too young for Barbie and that Mrs. Saffarian was allowing Karen to grow up too fast. She also didn't approve of Karen's pierced ears, which she said made Karen look "tough." I thought Karen's collection of earrings were pretty—especially the tiny ladybugs with the sparkling red ruby wings.

My mother had strong opinions about a lot of things. Sometimes I agreed with her. Other times I didn't.

"Wanna play kickball?" Karen thrust a large red rubber

ball in my hands. It was still light outside. Plenty of time left for a good game.

"Sure!"

Up and down the street, front doors slammed as the neighborhood kids came out to join the game. Newly paved, Fairview Road was perfect for kickball. Because it was a dead-end street (or what my mother preferred to call a *cul-de-sac,* which she said was a much nicer word) there was hardly any traffic. We positioned three rocks for the bases, and drew the pitcher's circle with chalk. Karen would pitch.

Linda Marshall, with her pale round face and short dark June Allyson bangs, played first base. Linda lived three doors down. Although Linda was quiet and not so athletic, I was glad to see her because there was always the chance she might be accompanied by her older brother Teddy. Teddy was kind of shy and unathletic, too, and his ears stuck out like *Mad* magazine's Alfred E. Neuman. But for some unfathomable reason I had a huge crush on him. My mother didn't appreciate the silly parodies and satiric pop-culture humor of *Mad.* When it came to magazines, she liked *Vogue, McCall's,* and *Better Homes and Gardens.* She was always clipping out recipes, especially for casseroles that included Cream of Mushroom and Cream of Chicken Soup, and trying them out on my father and me. One of her favorite recipes was a dish called "Chicken and Rice," which consisted of Minute Rice topped with warmed-up Cream of Chicken Soup, right out of the can. She said it was "quick 'n' easy—plus delicious!" I agreed. But sometimes it made me a little bit thirsty.

Second base was Suzie D'Agostino, who lived at the bottom of the street in a rambling old farmhouse. Suzie was a year younger than I—eons when you're in the fourth grade—and her father was the builder of all the new homes on Fairview Road. Mr. and Mrs. D'Agostino had lots of kids— I wasn't sure how many—and a big yard with a small barn and a chestnut-colored horse. My mother didn't approve of the D'Agostinos' outdoor clothesline. "All those clothes flapping in the wind," she said. "It's an eyesore. It makes a bad first impression and brings the whole neighborhood down."

Third base was Mikey Hogan, who liked to blow up frogs with cherry bombs.

Playing outfield with me was delicate fair-haired Nigel Witherspoon. Nigel's mother was English, and spoke with an actual British accent, and she had a dramatic white stripe running down the middle of her long, straight jet-black hair. Mrs. Witherspoon was *divorced*—the word was always whispered. Of all the neighborhood moms, my mother seemed to have a soft spot in her heart for Mrs. Witherspoon. One day I asked her why. "It's not easy having a child and being divorced," she said. But she didn't whisper. She said the word loud and clear. *Divorced.*

Finally, there was Eva Groutmann. The Groutmanns were of German descent, and buxom Mrs. Groutmann had once been a professional opera singer. Like her mother, Eva sang like a nightingale. And swore like a sailor. Eva and I didn't get along. Oh, things would go smoothly enough, until Eva would say something annoying, and I'd say, "Knock it *off*." And then Eva would call me a curse word, and I'd say, "*Shut* up!" And then Eva would say, "Drop *dead!*" and suddenly the two of us would be rolling on the ground in a ball of dust fighting like alley cats.

Eva had a big, beefy brother in the eighth grade named Bucky. I didn't get along with him, either. Bucky was a bully. When we gathered at the bottom of the street to wait for the school bus, Bucky teased the smaller kids. Sometimes he'd hit them on the head with his school books, bringing them to tears.

One night when I complained to my mother about Bucky, she said, "You've got to learn to fight your own battles." She was busy washing dinner dishes, and I thought our conversation was over, so I turned to leave the kitchen.

"Wait," she said.

"What is it?" I asked.

"Listen to me, Kitty," she said. "There will always be bullies in life. If Bucky bothers you so much, stand up to him." For someone so concerned about outward appearances and "what other people might think," my mother's no-nonsense attitude toward bullies took me by surprise. She seemed to speak from experience.

"When you were growing up did you ever know a bully?" I asked.

"When I was growing up?" she repeated. For a moment she was silent, and then she shook her head. "No," she said, "not when I was growing up."

"Well then, how do you know so much about bullies?" I asked.

"Oh, Kitty," she replied, "why do you ask so many questions?" She sighed. "It was all so long ago. All I know is that when you find yourself in a bad situation, you can't waste a minute's time. You've just got to do what you have to do to take care of yourself." She turned and plunged her yellow rubber gloves back into the sudsy dishwater.

One cold snowy morning at the bus stop, Bucky was up to his old bullying tricks, teasing the little kids and bonking them on the head with his books. The time had come to take my mother's advice. I backed up twenty feet, paused . . . and sucked in a deep breath of icy air. When I exhaled, steam surged out of my nose and mouth like a snorting bull. Then I charged—crashing head-on into Bucky at what felt like fifty miles an hour.

Bucky hit the pavement hard. His books went flying, along with the contents of his Lone Ranger lunch box. A red apple bounced wildly and tumbled down the street as though trying to run away from the scene. For a moment there was stunned silence. And then, to everyone's amazement, Bucky started crying. I almost felt bad for what I had done. Almost. Later, when I told my mother what had happened, she said I had done the right thing.

And she was right. Bucky never bothered the little kids again.

BEFORE WE KNEW IT, our game of kickball was over. The evening sky had changed from lavender to deep purple. Beneath a crescent moon, a single star hung as though suspended by an invisible thread. The windows of the houses on Fairview Road glowed softly, and under the front porch lights the silhouettes of mothers and fathers appeared, calling their children home. In the distance I heard my mother's silver whistle . . .

"SWEET DREAMS, SCOOTER." My father's tall, broad frame filled my bedroom doorway.

"'Night, Dad."

"Don't stay up too late."

"Okay."

Wearing a faded flannel nightgown, I knelt to examine the contents of my bookcase—three crowded shelves carefully alphabetized by title, with the exception of bothersome articles like "the" and "a." I loved my books—their musty

smell, the creamy texture of the pages, and the illustrations—
especially the color frontispieces protected by translucent
gossamer tissue. I loved reading . . . the power of the words to
instantly transport me to faraway worlds . . . the way it felt
when my moistened index finger gripped and turned each
page. With my sister gone away to college, sometimes the
house could get pretty quiet and lonely. Books were the big
noisy family I sometimes longed for. Books were my friends.

Tilting my head to read the titles, I let my fingers
travel along the books' worn and tattered spines . . . *Alice's
Adventures in Wonderland* . . . *The Borrowers* . . . *Charlotte's
Web* . . . *A Child's Garden of Verses* . . . *Eloise* . . . *Five Little
Peppers and How They Grew* . . . *Hans Brinker or the Silver
Skates* . . . *Heidi* . . . *Little Women* . . . *The Magical Mimics
in Oz* . . .

My hand came to rest on *The Secret in the Old Clock*,
the first book in the Nancy Drew mystery series. Just what
I was looking for. I practically knew the story by heart:
Nancy Drew, the plucky teen sleuth in her blue roadster,
finds the clue to the whereabouts of an old will in a mantle
clock, enabling the poor and struggling heirs to receive
their rightful inheritance.

Book in hand, I climbed into bed. As if on cue, Roxie
appeared and pushed her nose under the crook of my
elbow. I patted the side of the bed and up she jumped,
curling herself into a warm furry ball at my feet.

Ten or fifteen minutes into the story, the words on the page began to blur. My head nodded. The book dropped to the floor. Too tired to say my bedtime prayers, I reached for the lamp on my nightstand and turned out the light.

Pulling the comforter up under my chin, I wiggled my toes.

"'Night, God." I murmured sleepily.

Good night, I thought I heard Him reply.

Or maybe it was just a dream.

The Secret in the Breakfront

THE OLD BREAKFRONT in our living room was my favorite piece of furniture. Burnished walnut, with tall glass doors, it took up an entire wall. With its graceful gothic styling and shelves of glittering treasures, it reminded me somehow of a church. From behind the glass doors, my mother's antique silver tea service and collection of compotes and candy dishes sparkled in the afternoon sun. The faceted crystal stopper on the Waterford decanter cast hundreds of tiny glittering rainbows dancing on the ceiling.

What I liked best about the breakfront was the top drawer, which wasn't a drawer at all, but a foldout writing desk, with seven cubbyholes filled with stamps, rubber bands, tiny pencils for recording bridge scores and—if I was lucky—a silver stash of foil-wrapped Hershey's Chocolate Kisses.

On this particular afternoon, I wasn't so lucky.

Instead of candy, there was something odd and out of place—as though hastily tucked in the drawer at the last minute—an eight-by-ten-inch official looking piece of paper with hand-calligraphy lettering and a tiny black-ink footprint. *A birth certificate.* The baby's mother was a woman named Bessie Mae Johnson Parker. The baby's father was a man named Edmund Parker. The baby was a girl: Carolyn Anne.

My sister's name was Carolyn Anne. But her last name wasn't Parker. It was Brinckerhoff, like mine. Likewise, my mother's maiden name was Bessie Mae Johnson. But her name wasn't Parker either. It was Brinckerhoff, like my father's name. *So who were these Parker people?* None of it made any sense. The fact that the Parker baby's date of birth matched my sister's birthday was especially troubling.

I took the sheet of paper and ran to my mother, who was unpacking groceries in the kitchen.

"Mom, what is this?"

Frowning, she snatched the certificate from my hand.

"Don't be a snoop," she snapped.

That shut me up. A snoop was the last thing I wanted to be. This was because *"Don't be a snoop"* was high on the list of my mother's top five maxims, which also included:

"Remember, you represent the Brinckerhoff family."

"Only a fool tells all he knows."

"Know when to leave a party."

And, finally, the decidedly more upbeat *"When you're feeling blue, count your blessings and do something nice for somebody else."* Although I hoped this didn't mean that every time my mother did something nice for someone else, which was quite frequently, it was because she was feeling blue.

I WAS CONFUSED. A few weeks earlier when I had found my father's love letters to my mother written before they were married, she hadn't called me a snoop. In fact, she had seemed rather delighted.

"Where in the world did you find these?" she had asked. Her voice was high and girlish and her blue-green eyes sparkled as she fingered the three-inch stack of flimsy tissue envelopes marked "AIR MAIL," and "PAR AVION."

"In the basement," I said. "At the bottom of a box of old photo albums."

She sighed.

"Your father wrote the best letters," she said. "It's the reason I married him."

The letters were very lovey-dovey. For fear of being called a snoop, I didn't tell my mother that I had read them all. Each letter began with "Bess Darling" and ended with "Yours Forever." I had heard my father call my mother "Sweetheart" and "Honeybunch," but "Bess Darling" was something new.

When World War II broke out, my father had enlisted in the Navy, where he served as a crew member on the Air Transport Service planes that flew in and out from Dinner Key in Miami, Florida, to the U.S. Naval Air Station in Guantanamo Bay, Cuba. In one letter he wrote about having a pet monkey and training a myna bird to say "Pretty boy." But mostly he wrote about how much he loved and missed my mother, and how he couldn't wait to get married, and how long it had been since he'd kissed her.

The way I'd heard it told, my parents had known each other since childhood.

My mother grew up in Niagara Falls, New York, where her family lived next door to an older retired couple, the Brinckerhoffs, who were my father's grandparents. Every summer when my father and his twin sister Mary Louise were growing up, they would travel from their home in Lansdowne, Pennsylvania, to Niagara Falls, to visit their Brinckerhoff grandparents—and play with the Johnson children who lived next door.

My mother told me that Dad's sister Mary Louise was her *best* summertime friend—and the reason why my middle name was Louise. My mother said that when she was a girl, she didn't have much interest in my father, who was known as a bit of a prankster—especially when he got in cahoots with her two brothers. She said that my dad was the reason for my grandmother's gray hair, what with his fake bottles of spilled ink, and the way he liked to turn the sprinkler on when she wasn't looking.

Over the years, the Johnson and Brinckerhoff families kept in touch. My mother went away to Syracuse University, where she majored in English. My father and his twin sister Mary Louise went to the University of

Maryland, where my father also learned how to fly small-engine airplanes. My father loved flying. Indeed, he loved everything about aviation, an industry which was, excuse the pun, just beginning to take off.

The way I'd heard it told, it was my mother's younger brother who told my father that his old childhood friend Bessie Johnson had moved from Niagara Falls to Miami, and that maybe he should look her up. I was a little fuzzy about exactly what prompted my mother to move to Miami, but whatever the reason, that's where she and my father re-met, and fell in love, and got married in 1944 at an old stone church in Coconut Grove. Because it was wartime, my mother's parents didn't attend the wedding. My father's parents traveled all night by train, sitting on their suitcases the whole way, to get there. My mother said she was so nervous that she lost her voice for two days.

That's the way I'd heard it told.

I never could find any pictures of my parents' wedding day. But I loved the black and white snapshot of the two of them, with my father so young and skinny in his white sailor suit and hat, and my mother in her short summer dress and open-toed shoes, with palm fronds blowing in the tropical breeze. Taken by my father around the same time was my mother's favorite photograph of little three-year old Carolyn, daintily bending to smell a pretty flower . . .

Now my mother adjusted her glasses and peered at the birth certificate.

"This is none of your business," she said. But she must have sensed my concern, because she placed her cool hand on my shoulder, looked me in the eyes and said, "And it's certainly nothing for *you* to worry about." Then she handed me the piece of paper and sighed. "Now go put this back where you found it."

But I *was* worried.

I returned to the living room and placed the document in the breakfront. As I closed the top drawer, I tried to reassure myself by going over the facts of our family that I knew to be true: Mom was my mother. Dad was my father. Carolyn was my sister. Despite the mysterious birth certificate, for now that was all I should know. Moreover, I was not a snoop.

Well, actually I *was* a snoop.

No matter.

Whatever the secret in the breakfront might be, I was determined to push it out of my mind.

That night, I tossed and turned, unable to sleep. I turned on my bedside lamp and crept over to the bookcase where my hand came to rest on *Shirley Temple's Story Book*, a Christmas gift from my Aunt Mary Louise. An oversized, lavishly illustrated anthology of classic fairy tales and legends, it was one of my favorite books.

There was only one problem. In the book was an illustration so scary that I always skipped past it, closing my eyes. Not only did I avoid looking at the picture, I even avoided *touching* it. The picture that filled my heart with fear was Arthur Rackham's ghoulish rendering of the headless horseman for Washington Irving's *The Legend of Sleepy Hollow*. Other illustrators depicted the horseman's "head" as a harmless pumpkin. But not Rackham. In Rackham's drawing, the horseman's head was *real*—disembodied yet still *alive*—bug-eyed and screaming with horror. It was the unnatural, disordered nature of the picture that I found so disturbing. Living heads were supposed to be attached to living bodies. What scared me most was the horseman's obvious, awful self-awareness of his plight—and his helplessness to do anything about it.

I pulled the book off the shelf and onto my lap.

Tonight will be different, I thought. *Tonight I will look at the picture.*

My heart beating wildly, I turned to the forbidden page. Determined not to blink, I fixed my eyes on the terrifying illustration of the headless horseman riding his black flaming steed while holding his severed head high in the dark night. To my dismay, he stared right back at me, and I could almost hear his anguished cry . . . "*Help me!*"

Taking a deep breath, I extended my trembling finger and—*touched* the picture!

Slamming the book shut, I jumped up, ran back to bed and pulled the covers up over my head. My heart was pounding so loudly I was afraid it would wake up my parents sleeping across the hall. I had faced the headless horseman and survived. But instead of feeling relieved or triumphant, I was filled with dread.

Something bad is going to happen, I thought. *Something very, very bad.*

With the discovery of the birth certificate in the breakfront, my world had been turned upside down and inside out. The fact that things were out of order, and that things might not be as they seemed, scared me to death. Now, I had a lot more to worry about than a scary picture in a children's book.

And there was nothing I could do about it.

A New Companion

SITTING AT THE TOP OF THE STAIRS, peeking through the balustrades, I watched my parents glide across the kitchen floor to the haunting strains of Hoagy Carmichal's "Stardust." My parents loved to dance, and I loved watching them. Now, as they swirled and dipped and swayed, it was clear they were as crazy for each other as when my father wrote his love letters.

At least I hoped so.

Since finding the birth certificate in the breakfront, I found myself not so sure about a lot of things.

What if, I worried, *my happy family was not as it seemed? What if Mom had once been married to someone else? What if Carolyn wasn't really my sister? And if all these things were true, what other secrets might my parents be hiding?*

As weeks passed and I tried to push away worrisome thoughts about the mysterious birth certificate, I gradually became aware that in addition to Roxie I had a new, unwelcome companion. Unlike my dog, this companion gnawed at me from the inside, twisting my stomach into knots and setting my heart racing. Sometimes, when I was busy at school, or playing with friends, or lost in a good book, it would leave me alone. But it always returned—chronic, vague and menacing. On the sunniest days it lurked inside me like a storm cloud, threatening to steal my joy. Irrational and unpredictable, it had a name: Anxiety.

Now it seemed there was always something to worry about.

One day I noticed a new freckle on my nose. I'd recently read in *Reader's Digest* about something called skin cancer. *What if I have skin cancer too?* I worried. A few days later, I noticed something white and wriggly in Roxie's poop. I told my father, and he took Roxie to the vet. When he came home from the vet, he said that Roxie would have to take medicine for something called "worms." *What if I have worms too?* I worried. When I told my mother about my fears, and she told me to stop being such a "worry wart," I worried that all my worrying was going to give me warts!

ONE SUNDAY MORNING we were invited for brunch at the home of a family named the Barkers. When Mr. and Mrs. Barker met us at their front door, they wore big smiles and seemed nice enough. Mrs. Barker showed us to the dining room, where she had prepared a sumptuous buffet with deviled eggs sprinkled with paprika, a clove-studded ham garnished with pineapple rings and maraschino cherries, green bean casserole topped with canned onion rings, and a fluffy angel food cake.

But as I moved around the dining room table and filled my plate, I realized there was something about the name Barker that bothered me. Barker sounded a lot like Parker—the name on the mysterious birth certificate.

Barker . . . Parker . . . Barker . . . Parker . . .

Like a skip on a record, the names repeated themselves over and over in my head. Suddenly, my heart began to pound and I felt my stomach doing flip-flops.

Mr. Barker was a professional cartoonist, a big man with a booming laugh. Standing next to his chair, I looked over his shoulder as he doodled on a cocktail napkin and entertained us with a funny story. Suddenly he stood up, roaring with laughter. As he stood, he accidentally knocked over the end table and his scotch on-the-rocks. Ice and broken glass scattered everywhere and I panicked. Bursting into tears I ran and hid under the dining room table. Nothing my parents would say could get me to come out. I felt terrible, because I knew I was embarrassing them with my behavior. All I could think of were the names on the birth certificate. I tried to think of something else, but the names kept repeating themselves over and over.

Barker . . . Parker . . . Barker . . . Parker . . .

The names scared me to death. As did Mr. Barker. I couldn't say for sure that Mr. Barker was drunk, but he sure was acting weird, and the thought that he *might* have been drunk was terrifying. I had no idea why. On television, drunkenness was supposed to be funny. Everyone laughed at the antics of Red Skelton's Willy Lump-Lump the Drunk, and Jackie Gleason's Reginald Van Gleason III, the perpetually soused top-hatted millionaire. I didn't. Sometimes these acts made me so uneasy I had to leave the room.

On the drive home, my parents asked me to explain why I'd gotten so upset.

"I'm sorry," I said. "I don't know."

Frowning, my mother took my hand and examined it closely. "When did you start biting your nails?" she asked.

"I don't know," I replied, pulling my hand away.

"You don't want to bite your nails," she said, shaking her auburn curls with disapproval. "It's not ladylike."

What I really wanted to do was to ask her about the birth certificate. What I really wanted was for her to stop looking at my nails, place her cool hand on my shoulder, look me in the eyes, and tell me again that the birth certificate was nothing for me to worry about. But I knew that even if she did all those things, I wouldn't believe her. I would still bite my nails. And I would still worry.

So I said nothing.

A FEW WEEKS LATER, on New Year's Day morning, I walked into the kitchen and found my father pouring whiskey from a bottle into his mug of black coffee.

"What are you doing?" I asked. I could feel the panic rising in my chest.

"Just enjoying a little Irish coffee," he replied. I thought I detected annoyance in his voice. It was a tone I'd never heard, as though what he really wanted to say was, "*None of your business.*"

"C'mon, Scooter," he said. "Lighten up. It's New Year's Day!"

He held the cup of spiked coffee high to greet the New Year.

Why do I feel so uncomfortable? I wondered. *So anxious that I have to leave the room?*

LOOKING BACK, I understand now how children—even very young children—are like sponges, capable of absorbing *everything* in their home environment. Over the next several weeks and months, fragments of long-ago overheard adult conversations, like whispering ghosts, flitted through my mind. Something about a first husband who was *a good man, until he drank* . . . about a woman taking her baby daughter and fleeing . . . about a wartime romance and a wedding on a warm January day. . . .

Eventually, I connected the dots. Eventually, I pieced

together all I had seen and heard over the years and grasped the essential facts: Before marrying my father, my mother had been married to another man who drank, with whom she had a baby girl. This meant that Carolyn was only my half-sister. Dad was her adopted father.

Maybe this is the reason that drinking scares me so much, I thought. *Maybe this is the reason I don't think drunkenness is funny*. Drinking was dangerous. Drinking had the power to change a good man to a bad man. Drinking had the power to break up marriages, even whole families.

Like Nancy Drew, I had successfully solved the secret in the breakfront.

Case closed.

But with the mystery solved, I felt no sense of satisfaction. Just sadness. And anger. I didn't want Carolyn to be my half-sister. I loved her too much. I wanted her to be my *whole* sister. I also felt a burdensome guilt about knowing something that I wasn't supposed to know and that I was forbidden to talk about to anyone. Not my sister. Not even my parents. If only my mother had simply and matter-of-factly told me the truth about our family. But she hadn't.

Now I had a secret too.

And my growing anxiety.

Fully roused, the unwelcome voice hissed in my ear.

My father drinks. That is a fact. I've watched him put

whiskey in his coffee cup with my own eyes. What if... what if Dad's drinking gets so bad that it someday breaks up our family too?

I tried to push away the thought. But like an irritating grain of sand trapped inside an oyster, the fear was fixed firmly in my brain.

Bugs and Bomb Shelters

AT DINNER I SAT as close as I could to my sister without falling off my chair. It was early summer and Carolyn had just returned home from her junior year of college. I was so happy to see her. The two of us tried not to giggle as we slipped tidbits of my mother's Cream of Mushroom Soup and Pork Chop Casserole under the table to Roxie.

"Great dinner, Bess," my father patted his moustache with his napkin. Then he cleared his throat.

"Kids," he said, "Your mother and I have some good news."

A baby! I thought. *We're having a baby!* So many of my friends had little brothers and sisters that I was always up for having a baby.

"We're moving to Miami," he said.

Okay. Not a baby. But—Miami!

My mind swam with travel poster images of palm trees, alligators and pink flamingoes . . . endless summer days spent frolicking in the ocean, building sand castles, munching coconut patties and sipping Shirley Temples with tiny paper parasols . . .

My mother was beaming. My dad had been promoted to General Sales Manager at National Airlines' company headquarters in Miami.

AS WE PULLED OUT OF THE DRIVEWAY in our packed station wagon, it seemed like everyone on Fairview Road showed up to say good-bye. The Saffarians were there, and the Marshalls, and the D'Agostinos, and Mrs. Witherspoon with little Nigel, and the Groutmanns. Even Bucky, who once he stopped being a bully turned out to be an all right kid, was there.

Holding Roxie close, I pressed my nose against the station wagon's rear window.

"Good-bye! Good-bye!"

Suddenly I felt an unexpected lump in my throat. Swallowing hard and blinking back tears, I waved and waved until our house was no bigger than a playing card and our friends and neighbors looked like tiny upright ants, antennas waving.

SOMEWHERE BETWEEN South Carolina and Georgia, my father told us about the house waiting for us in Miami. It was a rental house, he said, near a good elementary school. After we got settled, he and my mom would look

for a house to buy. Some of the houses in Miami had outdoor *lanais*, he said. Lanai was a Hawaiian word that
meant "garden patio." Many of the newer homes had
bomb shelters . . .

Bomb shelters? I wondered. *What kind of town is Miami
anyway?*

He rambled on . . . Our house had a carport and
three bedrooms and one and a half bathrooms. I had just
about dozed off when I heard the words "swimming
pool." Our house had a *swimming pool*! How tropical!
How exotic!

Well, our house did have a swimming pool. It also had
something else tropical and exotic. Our house had bugs.
Not just garden variety spiders, ants, or roaches—though
it had its fair share of those too. Our house was infested
with something called *palmetto bugs*, which were like
roaches, but bigger. Much bigger. Plus, they flew. Picture a
black Volkswagen beetle with wings.

This was war. On the first night in our new house, my
mother, sister and I armed ourselves with rolled up newspapers and devised a three-step plan of attack. First, we
turned off the bathroom light. Then we waited five minutes. Holding our breath as Mom reached into the darkened bathroom and flicked the light switch on, we
watched in horror as the walls literally moved with bugs.
Brandishing our paper weapons and screaming at the top

of our lungs, we moved in like a swat team and let the enemy have it.

That night, as I lay in bed, I momentarily panicked at the flicker of movement on my bedroom floor.

Thankfully, it was only a mouse.

WITH HIS NEW JOB IN MIAMI, my father was doing a lot less fishing and a lot more traveling. It was the dawning of the aviation industry's most glamorous era and National Airlines, with its new fleet of DC-8 fan jets and "Airline of the Stars" ad campaign, was leading the way. Part of his new job included a lot of business entertaining, including cocktail and dinner parties at our new air conditioned house with a "bird cage" screened-in patio and swimming pool.

My mother said her favorite part of entertaining was just before the guests arrived. That's when she would glide around the patio, past the blue shimmering pool, past the lush tropical planters illuminated with emerald accent lights, gracefully bending to light flickering votive candles and fragrant sticks of vanilla incense. She wore a glamorous full-length Hawaiian floral "float," and plastic jeweled Egyptian-style gold thongs that hooked around her middle toe and hugged her slim ankles. Viewed from above it looked like she was wearing sandals, but her feet were actually bare. My father said he thought they were sexy. My job was to be in charge of the crackers and potato chips, which my mother told me to put out at the very last moment because they so quickly went limp in the Florida humidity.

One night, when a party had ended and the last guest had gone, she leaned against the front door and said, "*Phew*. I'm glad *that's* over."

"Mom," I asked, "why do you say you're glad the party's over?"

"Oh, it's just that when it's *business*, you've got to weigh *every* word you say," She sighed. "You know. Office politics. It can be *exhausting*."

I wasn't exactly sure what she meant about office politics, but I gathered that being a corporate wife was not always easy. I can see now that my mother's identity, like so many women in the 1960s, was in large part obtained through the success of her husband—and her children. No wonder it was important that everything about her family be "under control" and "perfect." As far as she was concerned, my father's job, and therefore her life, depended on it. So she became a master of small talk, what my father affectionately called "the hostess with the mostest," with her sexy Egyptian barefoot sandals and lilting ice-cube laugh.

When she was in full hostess-mode, my mother genuinely seemed to have a good time. *But is it all an act?* I wondered. *And if so,* I worried, *what else is an act? Is she faking it when she smiles and is nice to me?*

I admired my mother and wished I could be so graceful and glamorous. But I was not. Passing trays of hors
d'oeuvres to party guests was not easy while at the same
time clumsily trying to hide my bitten nails.

AS I MENTIONED EARLIER, the boys and girls at my new elementary school in Miami were much more grown-up than
my friends back in Medfield. I wanted so badly to fit in. I
began taking off my socks when I got to school so I could
be like the other girls. Though with my rubber-toed Keds,
the look wasn't quite right. I was too embarrassed to ask
my mother if I could shave my legs. And I didn't need a
bra. But I did ask her to take me to the mall to buy me a
pair of Thom McAn dress-up flats.

"Are you *sure* this is what the girls are wearing?" she
asked, as she picked up the pointy-toed shoes and eyed
them critically. "They're a little grown-up, don't you think?
And not very practical."

I hated shopping with my mother. Though if I was
honest, the problem wasn't my mother. It was me. That is,
the problem was my *body*. I wasn't slender and curvaceous
like my classmates Katie and Geena. Not yet eleven years
old, I was young for sixth grade—thick around the middle
with skinny legs. It didn't help matters that since moving
to Miami, I'd put on weight. In Miami there were no more
woods to explore, no trees to climb.

One night I went with my parents out to dinner at a fancy restaurant called Joe's Stone Crab on Miami Beach. Dining at the table next to us was the popular late night TV talk show host Jack Paar with his wife Miriam and their daughter Randy, who was about my age.

Later, I overheard my mother talking to someone on the phone about the encounter.

"What a *fat little girl* Randy Paar is!" she exclaimed.

I winced. Self-consciously I pinched my soft doughy midriff. *Is that what Mom thought about me too?*

AFTER BUYING A PAIR of black flats at Thom McAn, we went to Sears, where my mother scanned the racks of "Chubbette" brand dresses in the plus-size girls' department.

"Try this on," she said, holding up an ugly black jumper. "It'll look good on you. Dark colors have a slimming effect, you know."

Maybe she thought she was helping, but she wasn't. I didn't want to have to wear special clothes that had a "slimming effect." I just wanted to be normal.

"Let's just go home," I said.

Waiting at home in the freezer was a fresh half-gallon container of cold, sweet, creamy macadamia nut crunch ice cream . . .

Just thinking about how good it would taste made me feel better.

AS THE MONTHS IN MIAMI PASSED BY, sometimes I felt awkward around my father, which was strange, because for as long as I could remember he'd always been my favorite go-to parent. I missed our father-daughter fishing trips, and I was getting too big to sit on his lap. One Saturday morning, I was so happy to see him that I spontaneously burst into a silly, childish uninhibited dance, like I used to do when I was little. But when I stopped twirling long enough to catch his smile, his expression was grim, and his blue eyes wide with alarm.

"Stop!" he cried. "Don't move!"

I followed his concerned gaze to the floor where inches from my bare feet, a tiny black scorpion waited, quivering with excitement. Its venomous tail was arched over its back, pointed directly at me, like one of Cuba's nuclear missiles.

Sometimes, I thought, *not even home is a safe place to be.*

THAT NIGHT I TRIED TO GO TO SLEEP by immersing myself in childhood memories of Medfield. But now I had to accept there was no going back. My childhood days of climbing trees, catching salamanders, and scrambling over stone walls were over. Never again would I go fishing with my father. Never again would I hear the sound of my mother's silver whistle calling me home.

I had thought Miami would be fun and exciting. But

all Miami had to offer was a busy mother who didn't seem to be able to hear me, a job that took my father away when I needed him most, a fat body, and a weird elementary school with a creepy teacher who would eventually be fired for being a sexual pervert. And the heat.

There was always the heat.

Turning to face the wall, I ran my thumbs back and forth across the ragged tops of my bitten nails. With every tender snag and rough spot, I felt a pang of anxiety and guilt.

The sun was coming up by the time I finally fell into a restless sleep.

Another Day in Paradise

WHEN I WAS VERY YOUNG, I talked to God. All the time. To do so was as natural as breathing. But the older I got, the farther away I seemed to drift from Him, until memory of our times together faded like a childhood dream. By the time I was in my early teens I hardly thought about God at all. Over the years, we had simply fallen out of touch. Too much time had passed without talking to keep the relationship alive.

Not that it mattered. We never had been much of a churchgoing family. In Medfield, I had attended Sunday school until the minister of our church ran away with Mrs. Spooner, a married lady in the congregation. It was quite a scandal.

The highlight of my religious education took place at the end of third grade when I received my official *Holy Bible with Helps*. "With Helps" meant maps and notes and six double-sided color plates with illustrations of Jesus when He was a boy among the elders in the temple; and Jesus with little children; and something titled *Ecce Homo* or "Behold the Man," which was a picture of the Roman magistrate Pilate gesturing to Jesus with an anguished expression that seemed to beg, "What in the world am I supposed to *do* with this man?"

On the same day I received my Bible, I discovered the spotted wing of a cecropia moth in a flowerbed outside the church. This was the closest I'd ever come to seeing a real cecropia moth—with its six-inch wingspan, the largest and most strikingly beautiful of all North American moths—and I carefully placed the fragile wing in the middle of my new Bible in the Book of Psalms. Every once in a while I opened the Bible to check to see how the wing was doing. At the end of seventh grade, when my father's twin sister Mary Louise died suddenly at the age of forty-six of a brain aneurysm, I opened the Bible to find that the wing had disintegrated into a powdery dust.

I hadn't opened the Bible since.

My father said he did his best communing with God early in the morning, preferably with a fishing rod in his hand. He also put a lot of philosophical stock in Rudyard Kipling's muscular nineteenth-century poem, "If," which he one day read to me out loud:

> *"If you can keep your head when all about you*
> *Are losing theirs and blaming it on you,*
> *If you can trust yourself when all men doubt you*
> *But make allowances for their doubting too . . ."*

The poem went on until it ended with the rousing promise: *"Yours is the Earth and everything that's in it; And—which is more—you'll be a Man, my son!"*

That last line was initially disappointing because, being a girl, I could never be a man, or my dad's son. But my father reassured me that the values in the poem made sense for everyone, including me. The poem offered a lot of wisdom for living, he said.

The poem may have offered a lot of wisdom for living, but it had nothing comforting to say about *death*, which I thought was too bad, because my father was deeply shaken when his twin sister died. They had always been very close—there was a palpable intimacy and sweet tenderness between the two of them. When my Aunt Mary Louise died, it was as though a part of my father died too. I didn't know it back then, but the bond between twins can be so strong that when one twin dies, the grief and sense of loss experienced by the surviving twin may be so acute as to trigger severe depression—sometimes even suicide.

A few weeks after Aunt Mary Louise's funeral, while attending a business meeting in New York City, my father said he felt dizzy and thought he was having a heart attack. Our family doctor told him that he had high blood pressure and that he should lose weight, stop smoking and drink less.

In Miami, my parents dropped me off at Sunday school, but seldom went to church themselves. In eighth grade, my Sunday school teacher made it clear that while the Bible was, indeed, a significant work of ancient literature, it was full of myths and superstitions, and one should never make the mistake of taking it seriously.

"So," I said to my parents on the drive home, "if the Bible isn't true, why should anyone go to church?"

They had no answer.

"Then I don't want to go anymore," I said. "It's a waste of time."

"Very well," my mother replied. "You don't have to go to church. But you'll have to do some community service instead."

For my mother, religion was about being kind and doing nice things for others, like baking cakes and cookies and taking them to friends who were "down in the dumps." I was already a volunteer Candystriper at a local hospital, so I changed my shift from Saturday mornings to Sundays, 9:00 AM to noon.

When I got home from my shift at the hospital, I looked forward to reading the Sunday comics, especially *Apartment 3-G*, a romantic soap opera about the adventures of Margo, Tommie and LuAnn, three beautiful working girls who shared an apartment in a big city. *Apartment 3-G* wasn't funny—but it reminded me of my sister, who had graduated from college and was now living and working in New York City. She had also fallen in love and was engaged to be married.

ONE SUNDAY AFTERNOON, after reading the comics, my eye was drawn to something called "Your Weekly Horoscope." According to my birthday, I was born under the sign of Sagittarius. My symbol was the archer. I was anxious about the upcoming week at school: a chapter exam in Algebra (a class I was barely passing), a paper due in English, plus an unrequited crush on blue-eyed Tommy Traynor, who sat in front of me in homeroom and looked just like Peter Noone of Herman's Hermits.

Good news, Sagittarians! the horoscope proclaimed. *This is your week to be confident in all things. Take on new challenges. The stars are in your favor. Romance looks good too.*

My heart raced with happiness. Soon I was getting up five minutes early to read the paper's daily horoscope before going to school, and eagerly looked forward to each month's new issue of *American Astrology* and *Horoscope* magazines. I saved my allowance and bought a copy of Linda Goodman's best-selling book, *Sun Signs*.

I was hooked. I liked the way astrology gave me an identity. Who was I? I was a *Sagittarian!* Enthusiastic. Idealistic. Like the archer, aiming high. The concept that something bigger than me was influencing, if not controlling, my destiny was somehow comforting. I especially liked the idea of having secret knowledge about the future. When anyone asked me what my religion was, I replied that I was a Sagittarian.

I WAS THIRTEEN YEARS OLD and in the ninth grade when my sister got married at the home of my grandparents in Niagara Falls. I adored Carolyn and was thrilled that out of all her friends and cousins, she had chosen me to be her maid of honor. I especially loved my full-length bridesmaid dress, which was gold brocade on top and maize-colored crepe on bottom, with matching gold-dyed squashed heels. The dress had an empire-style waist, which my mother pronounced "*ahm-peer*," and said was "very flattering," which meant that it concealed my pudgy midriff.

Things were going great until the night before the wedding, after the rehearsal dinner, when my mother took me aside, sat me down on my grandmother's green sofa and said, "Kitty, there's something I think you should know."

And that's when she finally told me about how she had been married once before, and had Carolyn, and then got divorced, and then fell in love with and married my father—all of which lead up to the big wedding-eve news that Carolyn was actually my half-sister.

"Why are you telling me all this *now*?" I snapped

angrily. "I've known about it for *years*. I figured it out long ago. I even asked you about it when I was little. When I found the birth certificate. *Remember?* Why didn't you tell me the truth then? Why did you keep it a secret?"

"We were living in such a small town," my mother replied. "It all happened so long ago, and we didn't think it was anybody's business."

"But I'm not just anybody!" I cried.

I was as sad and angry as when I had been a little kid. I didn't want my sister to be my "half-sister." I loved her too much. I wanted her to be my *whole* sister. Especially tonight, on the eve of the biggest day in her life. Why in the world would my mother choose *now*, of all times, to tell me something she should have told me long ago?

Shaking my head with disgust, I got up from the sofa and walked away.

IN NINTH GRADE my best friend was a girl named Pam Moran. I couldn't figure out what she saw in me. Pam had a beautiful figure and wore all the latest fashionable name-brand clothing—Villager A-line skirts, Capezio flats, and Ellen Tracy pastel long-sleeved collarless blouses. With her straight yellow pageboy and perfect Cher bangs, she could easily be mistaken as one of Miami Palmetto (yes, like the bug) Junior High School's popular girls. I, on the other hand, was potato-shaped, with unruly bangs and altogether unremarkable dirty blond hair that frizzed in the Florida humidity.

After school, Pam and I would walk to her house and make Peter Pan peanut butter and Welch's concord grape jam sandwiches, and spend hours listening to *Rubber Soul*, the Beatles' just-released album—all the while dreaming of forming a girl band of our own. We would call our band the "Modrians," a play on the English slang word "mod" and the Dutch artist Piet Mondrian, whose modernist paintings had inspired Yves Saint Laurent's classic sixties red, blue, black and white sleeveless shift. We sketched endless versions of our album cover, with Pam on drums and me on bass wearing Mondrian-style dresses with short white go-go boots. Pam practiced on her older brother Jake's drum set. For fifteen dollars I bought a used bass guitar with a cracked neck, and taught myself to pick out the chords to the Animals' "House of the Rising Sun." It didn't matter that our musical skills never reached a level that enabled us to successfully play a single song. It was the teenage dreaming and fantasizing that was so much fun and that bound us so intensely and inextricably together.

One afternoon after school, the hours slipped away until the grandfather clock in the Morans' living room chimed six times. Moments later, Pam's pink princess phone jingled.

"Hello?" Pam answered. Grimacing and widening her eyes, she handed me the receiver. "It's for you."

"Where *are* you?" my mother asked.

"You know where I am," I said. "You're the one who called."

"Don't be fresh." She was furious. "Do you have *any* idea what time it is? I want you home *now*. Your father is here, and he wants you home too."

My parents didn't like Pam. My father didn't like her because whenever their paths crossed, Pam didn't look him in the eyes. My father always said you can't trust someone who won't look you in the eyes. My mother didn't approve of Mrs. Moran because she worked full-time and the three Moran children came home after school to an empty house. They both agreed that Pam was a bad influence on me.

Truth be told, I was probably a bad influence on Pam. At school, my grades were slipping. At home, I was moody and disrespectful. I was still angry at my mother for her ill-timed decision to finally tell me about her first marriage on the eve of my sister's wedding.

It reached the point where my parents forbade me to go to Pam's house after school.

"She can come to our house when I am home," my mother said. "But you cannot go there."

This worked for a while, until one afternoon, close to the end of the school year. My mother was hosting a bridge party at our house, and I figured she wouldn't miss me . . .

PAM'S MOTHER HAD JUST COME HOME from work when I heard the sound of a car pulling in the Morans' gravel driveway. There was the squealing of brakes. A pounding at the door. It was my mother. Angrier than I'd ever seen her in my whole life.

"*You!*" She moved toward me and grabbed my arm. "How *dare* you disobey me? You are coming with me right now. *Home.* Where you belong."

With a curt nod of her head to a stunned Mrs. Moran, she dragged me out the door.

"How could you do this?" I cried in the car on the way home. "You've ruined my life. I—I—*I hate you!*"

She just kept on driving.

The five-minute ride home seemed more like five hours as the two of us rode in icy silence. I pressed my right shoulder hard against the passenger door to get as far away from my mother as I could and stared out the window. Sobbing, I watched the low-slung Florida houses and lush tropical foliage pass by. It was hard to believe that there were people, like my parents, who actually thought of Miami as paradise. I felt more like it was hell.

All I knew was that I was one fat, unhappy kid.

Counting Calories

A FEW WEEKS LATER, my father stood behind the turquoise and gold-flecked Formica bar by the pool and fixed his usual glass pitcher of after-work cocktails. He liked his martinis stirred, not shaken, no olive, poured into an old-fashioned glass. Tamping the unlit end of his cigarette on the glass-topped patio table, he motioned for me to come and sit next to him on the hibiscus print sofa.

WHEN I WATCHED how often and how much Dad was drinking, it worried me. Since Aunt Mary Louise's death, he had been drinking every night. As far as I could tell, he never actually got drunk. That is, his speech remained clear and he never became loud or belligerent. He poured his first martini when he came home from work, and from that point on he had a drink in his hand until he fell asleep in the den in front of the television. For my father, it seemed that alcohol served as an anesthetic, numbing some kind of pain from an invisible wound. Even so, I could always tell when there was alcohol in his system. I could see it in his eyes. It gave me the creeps and scared me. When he was drinking, part of him disappeared, replaced by something—or someone—else.

Many times I tried to talk to my mother about my father's drinking. When I did, her eyes clouded, and for a moment I thought she winced, as though thinking about the subject physically hurt. Then, with a quick shake of her head she would say, "Don't be silly. Your father works hard. He's just unwinding after a long day." When I visited my sister at her apartment in New York and mentioned it to her, she said, "You worry too much. Dad's fine." So I stopped mentioning it. But I watched in silence as he drank more and more and more. At night I lay in bed awake, waiting for my father to finally get up from the sofa in the den, turn off the television and go to bed. Not until I heard the click of the bedroom door could I go to sleep too.

"WHAT'S UP?" I sat next to my father on the sofa.

"Well, Scooter, it's time you and I had a talk," he said. "Next year you'll be entering tenth grade and starting high school. You've expressed unhappiness about your weight for a long while. The time has come to face facts: Baby, you're fat."

His lips continued to move, but the roaring in my head was so loud I couldn't hear what he was saying. *Fat?!* I wanted to scream. *Well, so are you! Plus you drink way too much!* But I was too upset to speak. Devastated. I never knew the truth could hurt so badly. Once, while walking home from school, two little kids had pointed at me and giggled. "You're *fat*," one of them had snickered. That had hurt. But hearing the same words from my father hurt much more.

My mother appeared from the kitchen where she had just skewered several chunks of red marbled beef and brightly colored vegetables onto a shiny brass kabob spear.

"What your dad is trying to say," she said, wiping her hands on her apron, "is that maybe now, over the summer, would be a good time to do something about your weight. High school is an opportunity for a fresh start."

THAT NIGHT I RESTED MY HEAD on Roxie's warm chest and listened to the rhythm of her beating heart, recalling the times as a child when I had rested my head on my father's chest. Now, instead of the low rumble of my father's laughter, I heard the low grumble of Roxie's stomach. Still, in its way, it was comforting and reassuring. While the passage of time had altered so many things, Roxie remained the same. She was my last surviving link to happier days.

THE NEXT MORNING I tagged along with my mother to the Publix Super Market. At the checkout line, I spotted a fifty-cent Dell pocket book titled *Count Your Calories*. According to the little book, the secret to weight loss was so beautifully simple as to be summed up in two sentences:

"One pound of body weight equals 3,500 calories. Burn more calories than you consume, and you are guaranteed to lose weight."

My mother said that before starting a diet, I should talk to our family physician, Dr. Herbert Allen. So I did. Dr. Allen asked me if I wanted to take pills to help me lose weight, and I said no, I wanted to do it on my own. Then he handed me a sheet of paper with a list of foods to avoid and recommended a diet of one thousand calories a day.

So I started counting calories. Every day. I liked counting calories. I couldn't control world events, or my success at a competitive high school, or my father's drinking, or the seemingly unbridgeable gap that separated my mother and me.

But I could control my weight.

Over the summer, I kept track of everything I ate in a small spiral-backed lined notebook. I learned to shun butter, mayonnaise and ice cream, and to love green beans, cantaloupe and nonfat cottage cheese. By the start of the new school year I had lost twenty-five pounds. On the first day of tenth grade, a popular boy said, "Wow, I almost didn't recognize you." I blushed with delight.

The only negative side effect of my weight loss was that I stopped having my period. I felt embarrassed about mentioning this to my mother, but when I did, she didn't seem too upset.

"You'd better go see the doctor," she said. "Just to make sure you're okay."

In the week leading up to the doctor's appointment, I started worrying about *why* my period had stopped. When suddenly, in the middle of the night, I sat bolt upright, gripped by a totally irrational fear.

What if I'm pregnant?

Intellectually, I knew the possibility of my being pregnant was absurd. I'd never even held hands with a boy. But it was a fear I couldn't shake. All I could think of was the rumor about how swimming with a boy could get a girl pregnant. I'd gone swimming with my next-door neighbor, a teenage boy, more times than I could remember.

What if I'm pregnant?

Don't be silly, I told myself. But like a broken record, the agonizing question repeated itself over and over in my head.

I turned on the light and tried to reassure myself that I wasn't pregnant by reading and rereading the pamphlet that my mother had given me when I got my first period, *Growing Up and Liking It,* written by the public relations department of a feminine products company. But the pages were mostly filled with anatomical drawings of the female reproductive system, with information about ripening eggs and fallopian tubes and (*Yuck!*) blood flow, all the while extolling the absorbent supremacy of their particular brand of sanitary napkins. There was nothing in the pamphlet about getting pregnant by swimming with a boy.

DR. ALLEN'S RECEPTIONIST was a bespectacled middle-aged lady with short cropped salt-and-pepper hair named Miss Bean—who also happened to be his mother. I had once overheard my mother describe Dr. Allen as "a bit of an odd duck, blunt to a fault with absolutely no bedside manner." He was chubby, with dark spiky hair and puffy eyes. Now he narrowed them to black slits, and listened as I told him how my diet had been successful, but how—I took a deep anxious breath—my period had stopped.

Dr. Allen leaned back in his chair, folded his hands, and pressed his two index fingers together in the shape of a church steeple.

"Well, Kitty," he said. "I'm sorry to have to tell you this. There's only one thing that could explain your period stopping."

My heart pounded, and I felt like I couldn't breathe.

"You're pregnant," he said.

"*No!*" I cried, bursting into tears. *Oh, God*, I thought. *What will my mother think? And what will we do with the baby? Will I have to drop out of school?*

Suddenly Miss Bean burst through the doorway. Her face was red, and she was furious.

"Herbert Allen," she scolded. "I heard every word you

said. You should be *ashamed* of yourself, getting this nice young girl all upset!"

Dr. Allen looked at me sheepishly. "I'm sorry," he said. "I was just kidding. Here," he scribbled a prescription. "This is for birth control pills. They'll get your period going regular again."

Why would Dr. Allen play a trick on me like that? I wondered, as I rushed past him in a blur of tears and confusion.

In the car on the way home I told my mother what had happened, but I left out the part about my secret fear that I might be pregnant. It was too embarrassing.

"Well, I don't think what Dr. Allen did was one bit funny," my mother said after hearing my story. "I agree with Miss Bean. He should be ashamed of himself." She shook her head. "I always thought he was an odd duck."

We stopped at a red light.

"And as for you," she said, "I want you to stop frowning. If you keep frowning like that, you're going to get a big ugly wrinkle on your forehead." She shook her head. "You worry too much."

She was right about that.

The Manatee

NEW HOUSES were springing up everywhere in southwest Miami, many along freshly dug canals carved out of coral rock. One day, while walking home from school, I heard a splash, as though someone had tossed a pebble in the water. I looked around but saw no one. Another splash. I peered into the canal.

A manatee!

I'd never seen a manatee before. This one was huge, floating in the canal's murky green water like a giant gray sweet potato. Her broad, flat paddle-shaped tail moved slowly up and down, keeping her massive snout just above the water. She swam so close I could see tiny bright droplets of water clinging to her whiskers, and she regarded me warily with dim water-colored eyes.

In the water, the manatee was a graceful dream, an aerodynamically-designed wonder, perfectly adapted to her environment. Her days and nights were spent mostly eating and napping. I'd read somewhere that a manatee consumes ten percent of its hefty tonnage—an average of one hundred pounds of aquatic vegetation, or ten thousand calories a day—just to survive. I was consuming calories too—1,500 a day, to be exact—just to survive at Miami Palmetto Senior High School, where I was in my junior year.

Unlike the manatee, I could not be accurately described as a graceful dream. But for two years I'd successfully kept off my excess weight, and was down to a svelte size eleven. Although I was still not small enough to shop at the mall's popular "5-7-9 Shop" (at five-feet ten inches tall, I never would be), but at least my days shopping in the "Chubbette" department at Sears were finally over. Now my top priority was to do everything necessary to keep the dreaded pounds from returning. Like a bizarro Scarlett O'Hara, I greeted each morning by mentally clenching my fist and shaking it at the sky. *With God as my witness*, I vowed, *I'll never be* fat *again!*

Oh, every once in a while I splurged and ate a "bad" food like ice cream, which triggered acute feelings of guilt and anxiety. But I learned to lower my caloric intake for the next few days to work it off.

Setting my school books on the sandy ground, I knelt at the canal's edge for a closer look at the manatee. *How*, I wondered, *did it ever find itself all the way to our suburban neighborhood?* I extended my hand to touch the tip of the manatee's nose, but it closed its nostrils and sank out of sight, leaving behind a shimmering necklace of green iridescent bubbles.

I picked up my books and continued walking.

When I arrived home, my mother was out shopping. I opened the refrigerator and scanned the contents . . . Diet Rite Cola, sugar-free cherry Jell-O, carrot and celery sticks . . . nothing too tempting. I opened the freezer door, and there it was: a brand-new unopened carton of macadamia nut crunch ice cream. My favorite!

Go ahead, I thought. *Fix yourself a bowl. You can cut calories and work it off tomorrow.*

I carried the bowl of ice cream out to the patio, and opened my Harper's Modern Classic edition of Aldous Huxley's *Brave New World*. I'd recently been reading a lot of science fiction and fantasy—Ray Bradbury's *The Martian Chronicles*, Daniel Keyes' *Flowers for Algernon*, Ambrose Bierce's *Occurrence at Owl Creek Bridge*, Robert Heinlein's *Stranger in a Strange Land*. But this book—with its compelling tale of John, "the Savage," and his quest for freedom and truth in a nightmarish dystopian future—was utterly captivating. Eagerly, I began to read:

> *From the bathroom came an unpleasant sound.*
>
> *"Is there anything the matter?" Helmholtz called.*
>
> *There was no answer. The unpleasant sound was repeated twice; there was silence. Then, with a click, the bathroom door opened and, very pale, John emerged.*
>
> *"I say," Helmholtz exclaimed solicitously, "you do look ill, John!"*

"Now I am purified," said John. "I drank some mustard and warm water."

They stared at him in astonishment. "Do you mean to say that you were doing it on purpose?"

"That's how the Indians always purify themselves," John said.

I stopped reading and thought of all the ice cream I had just consumed.

Was it possible, I wondered, *to make myself sick? To get rid of this ice cream and the wicked calories? To purify myself, like John?*

I mixed two big spoonfuls of French's yellow mustard in a tall glass of warm tap water and carried it to the bathroom where I swallowed it down, then stuck two fingers down my throat, and leaned over the toilet.

"What are you doing in there?" My mother knocked on the bathroom door. "Is everything all right?"

"Fine," I said, "Everything's fine."

In one sense everything *was* fine. More than fine. Everything was wonderful! Thanks to Aldous Huxley, I had actually discovered a way to achieve the impossible: How to *not* have my cake (and ice cream) and eat it too! Like John, I'd been purified—purged of the wicked calories. Though the whole process was revolting. And exhausting. I felt weak and faint. And vaguely guilty. If anyone ever found out what I had done, I would have been so embarrassed. Surely they would think I was crazy.

NEXT DAY, walking home from school, I stopped at the canal's edge and searched the murky green water for any sign of the manatee. But she was gone. All that remained was my own pale, watery reflection.

I tossed a pebble in the water and watched myself disappear.

Late Bloomer

"HEY, STRETCH! How's the weather up there?" A cute crush named Scott was actually slowing down to say hello while on his way to class.

"Uh-h-h." I fumbled with my locker, my cheeks hot with embarrassment. *Oh, dear God*, I panicked. *Help me say something. Anything!*

I needn't have worried. By the time I collected my thoughts, Scott was long gone down the hall. When it came to boys, I was not only too tall. I was clueless.

Like most high schools, ours had the usual sharply etched social strata. There were the jocks and the preppies. The brains and the nerds. The artists and the outsiders. But why make things so complicated? The way I saw it, Miami Palmetto High School was divided into two distinct camps: There were the kids who dated, and the kids, like me, who didn't.

One day I came across my mother's old diary, a small gilt-edged volume titled *Each Day's Doings*. When I read about her high school and college days—an endless whirl of parties, dances and adoring beaus—it seemed like something out of *Gone With the Wind*. While she was certainly no Southern belle, it was easy to imagine her tossing her red curls, flashing her azure eyes, and trilling coquettishly, "Well, *Fiddle-dee-dee!* I do declare I cannot decide which one of you boys I like best!"

Sometimes I wondered if my mother and I had been in high school together, would we have been friends? Or would I have been invisible to her? I liked to imagine that she would have been nice to me. Perhaps we would have studied together. Then again, she had been a straight-A student. I did all right in English and Art, but it was all I could do to get passing grades in Geometry and French. In the end, I guessed we probably wouldn't have been friends.

Now that I was a senior, and still had yet to be asked out on a date or to a prom, I worried that I disappointed her.

One Saturday morning she knocked at my bedroom door. She wore a yellow terrycloth towel twisted into a turban on her head and asked if I had time to "do" her just-washed hair. My mother said she liked the way I styled her hair better than the lady at the beauty parlor. I think she liked the price too. For fifty cents I combed a generous dollop of pink Dippity-Do styling gel through her hair and curled the damp tendrils around a dozen pink foam rollers. Then I sat her in a comfortable chair under my pale blue portable hard-hooded hair dryer. Even under the noisy dryer, thumbing through the latest issue of *Vogue*, she somehow managed to look glamorous.

I liked doing my mother's hair. And not just for the money. I liked doing her hair because it provided a rare opportunity for intimacy between us—a sense of connecting. I liked doing her hair because it was the one girly thing that we could enjoy doing together. There was no need to go shopping for prom dresses. And mother-daughter manicures were out of the question because I still bit my nails to the quick.

Forty-five minutes later, I lifted the hood and unfastened a roller. Dry as a bone.

"I think you're done," I said.

I unfastened the rollers and fluffed out the stiff, crinkly tube-shaped curls with my fingers. Using a narrow black comb, I vigorously teased her hair until it stood out around her face like a fright wig, which made us both laugh. Then, with a soft bristle brush, I lightly smoothed the surface and gently tugged at her auburn curls so they framed her face—just the way she liked.

"Now cover your eyes," I said, shaking the can of Aqua Net Extra Super Hold hairspray.

As I sprayed her hair, the Beatles' "Eleanor Rigby" played on the radio.

"*O-o-oh*," she said, "there's that song I like. Can you turn it up?" My mother didn't enjoy most rock music, but there was something about this song with its lush strings and sad, haunting refrain . . .

All the lonely people, where do they all come from?

All the lonely people, where do they all belong?

"Mom?"

Our eyes met in the reflection of the vanity mirror.

"Remember back in Medfield, when Carolyn was in high school, and she went out on dates and to all her proms?" I asked. "Remember all her pretty dresses, and how the boys would come pick her up at the house and have to meet Dad first and shake his hand?"

Smiling, my mother nodded. "Yes," she said. "I remember. Those were happy days."

"Well—well—sometimes I wish it was like that for me," I said. "I mean, I'm sorry about the way I've never had a boyfriend—or even gone on a date. It's not—it's not that I don't *want* to . . ."

"Oh, Kitty," she replied. "Don't be silly. You don't want to grow up too fast." She smiled, lightly touching her slender neck just below the ear and turning her head to admire her finished hairdo in the mirror. "There's nothing wrong with being a late bloomer."

For a moment I relaxed, basking in the warmth of my mother's acceptance and approval.

"But I really do wish you'd stop biting your nails," she said. "Boys don't like girls who bite their nails."

Wincing, I thrust my hands behind my back.

I was ashamed and self-conscious about my stubby fingernails. I believed they were an outward visible sign of my true inner self, a betrayal of my chronic anxiety—not to mention my secret habit of stuffing myself with forbidden foods and then making myself throw up. *If Mom ever knew about that . . .* I shuddered.

She fished in her red ostrich leather change purse and handed me four shiny quarters.

"Thank you so much," she smiled happily. "No one does my hair like you."

I hardly noticed the generous tip. All I could see were my mother's healthy, manicured, unbitten nails.

What must it be like, I wondered, *to be so in control and perfect?*

Good-bye, Old Friend

FOR THE PAST SEVERAL DAYS, Roxie hadn't been her old self. On two occasions she had stumbled and fallen, and when we took her to the vet, he said she had suffered two small heart attacks. She had just taken a long drink from her water dish when her hind legs gave out and she collapsed in a heap for the third time.

"Roxie?" I looked up from the Saturday morning paper. "You okay, girl?"

Slumped against the sliding glass door in the kitchen, she looked up at me with frightened brown eyes.

"C'mere, girl." I patted my thigh. "You can do it. I know you can."

But this time, Roxie could not get up.

On the way to the vet, my father drove, and I sat in the back seat with Roxie spread across my lap. Her body was limp, and her breathing was shallow and rapid. Her eyes were closed, and her mask and muzzle, once velvety black, were flecked with silver. Roxie was fourteen—old for a boxer. I buried my face in her smooth butterscotch-colored fur and listened for her heartbeat, but it was so faint I could barely hear it.

Stretched out on the vet's cold stainless steel examining table, Roxie looked so tiny and frail. Not like herself at all.

When had she become so old? I wondered. I held her paw.

"I can give her some drugs," the vet said. "But her heart's shot. She might live a day or two. Maybe a week. I wish I had better news." He stroked Roxie's neck. "What do you want me to do?"

With tear-filled eyes I looked to my father, who returned my gaze with the saddest expression I'd ever seen.

This can't be happening, I thought.

"I know this is a difficult decision for you," the vet said. "But I can assure you she won't feel any pain. It will be as though she's going to sleep . . ."

"Scooter?" my father asked quietly. "I know how much you love Roxie. What do you think?"

But I was crying so hard I couldn't speak.

My father must have nodded his permission to go ahead and put Roxie to sleep, because the next thing I remember, his arm was wrapped around my shoulder and he was gently leading me out of the vet's office and toward the car.

On the way home I sat in the front seat next to my father. He handed me Roxie's empty collar and rolled up leather leash.

"She was a good dog," he said, steering the car onto the highway. "We did the right thing."

Overwhelmed by a tsunami of grief and loss, I nodded numbly. Roxie was my best friend, my last link to simpler, happier childhood days. Roxie didn't care if I worried too much, or bit my nails or stuffed myself with forbidden fattening foods and made myself throw up.

And now she was gone.

Surviving

WHEN IT CAME TIME TO CHOOSE a college, my parents had only two requirements: It had to be a state school, and it had to be located on a National Airlines route. So I chose the University of South Florida in Tampa.

Two weeks before going away to college, I felt a stabbing pain in my chest that wouldn't go away. In the middle of the night I worried that it was cancer. Or pleurisy. Or a heart problem. Or a tear in my esophagus caused by my secret bingeing and throwing up. *Oh God, what if it was that?*

I visited the doctor, who listened to my heart, took my blood pressure and then patted me on the shoulder. The pain in my chest was caused by nerves, he said, probably about leaving home and going away to college.

"Relax," he said. "Try not to worry so much."

MY PARENTS DROPPED ME OFF at my dorm room with my matching two-piece set of turquoise Samsonite luggage, make-up case, portable hairdryer and typewriter. My roommate had arrived earlier in the day, and her mother was busy bustling about the room hanging curtains, lining the drawers with paper, and spraying the room with Lysol.

Lingering outside the doorway, my father pointed to the dial on his wristwatch and raised his eyebrows at my mother as if to say, "Okay, let's get this show on the road."

In the car on the way to school, my parents had told me that after they dropped me off, they did not intend to stay. It was better that way, they said. They didn't want to "baby" me. Besides, it was a long drive home, and they had a cocktail party to go to that evening.

So we hugged each other and said good-bye. There was no fuss. No tears.

Maybe my parents are right, I thought. *Maybe it is better this way . . .* And then I had an unpleasant thought. *Maybe the real reason they're so eager to hit the road is so Dad can get home in time for a drink.*

BY NOW, my worst fear had come true. Although no one in the family wanted to admit it, my father *was* an alcoholic. Maybe it was easy to overlook his problem because so far, he was functioning well enough. Despite his drinking, his airlines career had continued to soar. Promoted to vice president of sales, he had been instrumental in launching National's coveted nonstop Miami-London route, and he traveled around the world opening offices in Tokyo, Rome and Frankfurt. But he drank every day. He used to wait until five o'clock in the afternoon for the day's first cocktail, but now he was drinking at lunchtime too. It had reached the point where the only way to be with my father when he didn't have alcohol in his system was to catch him early in the morning when it was still dark, and he sat out on the patio in his bathrobe and bare feet, wiggling his toes and reading the paper, and drinking his morning cup of black coffee. That's when his blue eyes were clear, and he was all there.

My mother's way of dealing with my father's drinking was to deny there was a problem. The alternative must have been simply too much for her to bear. I suspected that on some deep, subconscious level she had always feared that he—like her first husband—would become an alcoholic. Indeed, I believed this fear had been present in her from the first day of her marriage, and that I had picked it up from her, like a virus, back when I was a baby in her womb.

I guess I knew for certain that my father was an alcoholic the night we went to a cocktail party at the house of a family friend, and he became so intoxicated that my mother reached into his sports jacket pocket, removed his car keys and quietly asked me if I would drive us home.

It was the first time I had ever seen my father truly, classically drunk. His eyes were bleary and he was unsteady on his feet. His speech was slurred. As I took his arm and guided him toward the car, I looked back over my shoulder to see my mother saying good-night to our host and hostess. She wore a frozen smile, and I could hear her ice-cube laugh and lilting cocktail party voice, all sparkly and merry, as though nothing was wrong. But I knew she was humiliated. And so was I. For the first time in my life I was ashamed of my father, and it felt awful. I didn't *want* to be ashamed of my father. I wanted to be proud of him. I wanted to be able to trust him. I wanted to know that I could count on my father to take care of my mother and me and keep us safe. More than anything, I wanted to know that my father—given the choice— would choose us over alcohol. But this was something that he could no longer do, which made me brokenhearted, frightened—and *furious*.

"You make me *sick*!" I cried, blinking back tears as I steered the car north along the South Dixie Highway toward home. I slapped at my father's knee as though he were my errant child. "How could you embarrass us like this?"

"And *you*," I spun my head around and glared at my mother accusingly in the back seat. "Why do you keep denying that Dad has a drinking problem? Why do you put up with it? Why don't you *do something* about it?"

Tears filled her eyes, and she shook her head.

But I didn't feel sorry for her. I felt contempt. She was so *weak*. And so was my father. And so was I. I hated them both. And I hated myself. Let's face it: I hated us all.

What is wrong with us? I wondered, as I squinted against the bright lights of oncoming traffic. Each in our own way, we were just doing what was necessary to survive: My father drank. My mother looked the other way. I worried all the time, bit my nails, and binged and purged.

We were all such flawed and broken creatures. We all so desperately needed help. But none of us knew how—or whom—to ask. So we just blundered on, each in our own way, doing our best to push back the darkness and get by. Oh, on the outside—with the exception of sloppy nights like tonight—we looked pretty good. But on the inside, behind closed doors, we were a mess—incapable of honestly facing our true selves, terrified of the consequences of being found out.

After all, what would people think?

I WATCHED as my parents headed down the dorm stairwell, stopping at the landing to turn around for one last good-bye.

"We love you!" my mother called. "Don't forget to phone us!"

"I won't forget," I said, waving. "I love you too."

And that was the truth.

A lonesome hollow ache tugged at my heart, and for a moment I thought I might cry. But my homesickness quickly evaporated as I placed my *Webster's New Collegiate*

Dictionary on the bookshelf, and set my Smith-Corona student typewriter on my desk.

The truth was, I was relieved to finally get away from my parents. Maybe we'd get along better at a distance. Maybe things would be better at college.

Waiting for Godot

"WHAT? WHAT IS IT?" Sitting bolt upright in my bed, panic gripped my chest and for a moment I thought I couldn't breathe.

"Take it easy," my roommate said. "You're freaking me out. I just wanted to let you know I'm leaving for class."

"I'm sorry," I said. "I must have had a bad dream."

"I don't know," my roommate said. "Every time I wake you up, you look like you've just seen a ghost. Are you sure you're okay?"

"Yeah," I said, flinging back the covers, and swinging my legs over the side of the bed. "I'm okay."

Reaching across the dirty ashtray on the bedside table, my fingers grasped a warm can of Tab. I took a swig. Late for English Literature, there was no time for breakfast. I zipped up my bellbottom jeans, pulled a pale blue T-shirt over my head and draped a string of multicolored beads around my neck.

Books. Keys. Soda. Cigarettes. I was out the door.

Walking along the cement paths that crisscrossed the

campus like a spider web, I had to admit my roommate was right. I hadn't had a bad dream. I'd just let down my guard long enough for her to glimpse my anxiety. In the bright light of day—busy with classes, schoolwork and friends—I could hold it at bay. But it was always there— especially late at night—perched on my shoulder like a malevolent bird of prey waiting to snatch my imagination and carry it away to a dark inner world where every worst fear threatened to come true.

I liked to think I wasn't alone with my inner turmoil. After all, it was a tumultuous time in America. In response to an unpopular president and an unpopular war, the country was bitterly divided. There were, as Buffalo Springfield sang in "For What It's Worth," battle lines being drawn.

On college campuses across the nation there was anger and unrest. Our school was no exception, where Students for a Democratic Society organized weekly speeches, marches and antiwar protests, including one in 1970, when fifty-three students were arrested. That same year, students declared a strike in response to the killings at Ohio's Kent State and the Vietnam War—although I was a little unclear as to what the difference was between going "on strike" and skipping classes. Campus policemen were disparagingly referred to as "pigs," clueless guys were "male chauvinists" and numerous female students burned or threw away their bras—which, as far as I could tell, only served to delight a good number of the clueless guys.

Things were changing so fast it was hard to keep up.

When I had arrived at college as a seventeen-year-old freshman, co-eds were housed in separate dormitories with strict visitation rules and weekend curfews, which suited me just fine. I liked my privacy. Less than a year later, the curfews were lifted and men roamed the halls. "Make love, not war," "Do your own thing" and "If it feels good, do it," became the reigning credos of the day.

No longer a late bloomer, at long last I was dating—and making up for lost time. But when it came to morals regarding sexual behavior, there were no guidelines. For better or worse, we liberated gals and guys were making up the rules as we went along. Two of my closest girlfriends became pregnant. One got married. The other had an abortion. There was no right or wrong. No moral absolutes. Like Humpty Dumpty, the social order of my parents' generation had fallen and broken into a thousand pieces.

And there were drugs. Coastal Florida was a major point of entry for marijuana, speed, hashish, LSD and mescaline. Whatever anyone wanted was easy to get. The only reason I didn't try hallucinogens like LSD or mescaline was because I was certain, with my tendency toward anxiety, that I would be guaranteed a bad trip. I had already spent far too many nights alongside friends who were not at all happy to see the walls melting, or the Virgin Mary at the bottom of a swimming pool. The last thing my overactive imagination needed was hallucinogenic drugs. My substances of choice, therefore, were Boone's Farm Apple Wine, occasional pot, cigarettes and—always the most reliably satisfying—food.

When I was really stressed—at least once a week—I grabbed a handful of quarters and headed for the snack vending machine at the end of the hall. Back in my room, with the door securely locked, I binged on bags of Fritos corn chips and packets of cream-filled Zingers, which were like Twinkies with yellow icing, wrapped in cellophane packages decorated with Charlie Brown and the gang from *Peanuts*. Once I'd had my fill, I sneaked down the back stairs to the bathroom on the floor below where no one knew me and made myself throw up. Mustard and warm water were no longer necessary. Two fingers did the trick. While the binge-ing and purging temporarily relieved my anxiety, it left me feeling physically spent, ashamed and guilty. Every time I gave in to the urge, I promised myself that I'd never do it again. But I knew that I would. It was my deepest, darkest secret. *No one* knew. Not my roommate. Not even my closest friends.

Surely, I thought, *no one else in the world has ever engaged in such a bizarre compulsive behavior.* Sometimes I worried that I might be crazy.

One day I overheard a group of students gossiping

about another girl in our dorm who had been caught making herself throw up.

"Have you ever heard of such a thing?" one girl asked. "Isn't it just disgusting?"

"The ancient Romans did it all the time," a classics major volunteered.

"Really?" I asked, trying not to sound too interested.

"Yeah, they'd just eat and eat until they were stuffed, and then they made themselves throw up so they could eat some more."

"Gross," I said.

If they only knew.

Truth be told, I was relieved to learn that other girls made themselves throw up. Maybe I wasn't crazy after all. Sick, yes. But not crazy.

What troubled me most was a persistent, nagging sense of loneliness and emotional detachment. If one day I looked out my dorm room window to see that all the trees and buildings had turned upside down and the sky had suddenly turned yellow, it wouldn't matter. Nothing mattered.

At the far end of my dorm, beyond the vending machines, was the pay phone that I used to call home on Sunday nights. Last weekend I'd felt so lost and empty that I hadn't bothered to call. What was the point? Whatever help it was that I needed, I knew it was something my parents did not have . . .

MY ENGLISH LIT PROFESSOR dimmed the lights, and the big boxy television mounted on a metal stand in the front of the classroom flickered to life with the black and white telecast of Samuel Beckett's classic play, *Waiting for Godot*, starring Zero Mostel and Burgess Meredith as the hapless tramps Vladimir and Estragon, who spent their days waiting in vain for the arrival of the mythical Godot. The play was at times absurdly hilarious, but mostly achingly sad— a poignant portrait of human suffering. When the lights came up, the professor described the work as a masterly depiction of something called "existential despair."

"In Beckett's world there is no God. No love. No truth," he said. "Such things are human conceits, illusions, artificial constructs created to infuse our pointless lives with false but necessary meaning."

Talk about depressing!

Maybe that's what is wrong with me, I thought. *Maybe I'm suffering from existential despair.*

All I knew was that everything in my life had become totally unglued. Like Vladimir and Estragon, I was desperately hoping and waiting for someone to come and save me.

Bridge Collapse

IT WAS SUMMER BREAK after my freshman year at college, and it felt good to be home—back in my old bedroom with the rickety three-tiered bookcase filled with my collection of childhood books, back in my old double bed with its marshmallow soft mattress and familiar faded pink floral sheets. At the same time, there was something sad and bittersweet about being home. Having spent a year away at college, I sensed that from now on I would always be a visitor.

I was clearing the dishes from the dinner table when I felt a sudden unexpected surge of affection for my mother, accompanied by a deep desire to confide in and hopefully connect with her. I couldn't tell her *everything*, of course. I couldn't tell her about all the drugs and sex at school, or my battle with anxiety—or my secret problem with food.

So impulsively, I told her about seeing the movie *Waiting for Godot*, and how sometimes I felt like the characters Vladimir and Estragon—so lonely, empty and despairing. It wasn't exactly homesickness, I tried to explain. It was something bigger.

"Did you ever feel like that?" I asked. "When you went away to college?"

She frowned.

"Oh, Kitty," she said with an exasperated sigh. "You *think* too much." She shook her head with disapproval. "Boys don't like girls who think too much."

Not helpful, I thought. *Not the answer I was hoping for.*

In my mind's eye I saw the flimsy bridge connecting the two of us collapse, the frayed ropes and rotted wood slats tumbling into the bottomless canyon that yawned ever wider between us.

Suddenly my mother brightened.

"What about joining a sorority?" she asked. "Did you ever think of doing that? Back when I was at Syracuse, I had so much fun with my sorority. We girls had the best time. And it was a great way to meet boys."

So, I joined a sorority.

Being in a sorority was fun. And it *was* a great way to meet boys. But it didn't stop me from worrying. Or biting my nails. Or bingeing and throwing up. And it didn't fill up that lonely, empty hole in my heart.

Of course, I didn't share these thoughts with anyone.

Especially my mother.

Lost and Found

THE FIRST TIME I met Renee Bakke, she reminded me of sunshine. It wasn't just her carrot-colored hair, transparent blue eyes and open face sprinkled with freckles. It was the way she glowed with an inner joy that radiated outward in warmth and good cheer. Renee was not a phony. She was, quite simply, well adjusted and happy.

"Kitty!" she called, as I was walking back to the dorm from the dining hall. "Wait up!" Her cheeks were flushed from running.

"Hey," I said. "What's up?"

"There's a meeting tonight I think you might enjoy," she replied. "There's music and pizza, and a talk. Wanna come?"

"Sure," I said. If it was okay with Renee, it was okay with me.

On the way to the meeting, Renee mentioned that the meeting was being sponsored by a student Christian organization.

But isn't that just a little—old-fashioned? I wondered. Most of the kids I knew were interested in Eastern faiths.

When it came to religion, I was still a practicing Sagittarian. Every morning and night I read my daily horoscope, and I hoped one day to save up enough money to send away for a lifetime astrological chart prepared by a professional astrologer.

But the moment I walked into the meeting room, I felt at home. The kids were friendly. The student leader got my attention.

"I've got good news for you tonight," he said. "God is real. He loves you. He has a special purpose for your life. It's the reason you were born."

This is news to me, I thought. It was my understanding that God was *dead*.

The meeting ended with everyone sitting in a large circle, and the leader asking for something called "prayer requests."

Huh?

A girl spoke up and said she was having trouble forgiving a friend. A boy said he was worried about his mother who had just been diagnosed with cancer. And then a girl asked for prayers for her father who was an alcoholic. That really got to me, and for a moment I was afraid I might cry.

I was impressed by the candor of the kids—especially their willingness to *ask for help*. They didn't seem to care at all about what other people thought. But they did seem to sincerely care about each other. And when they took turns praying out loud, it was unlike anything I'd ever heard.

They didn't use prayer books or fancy language. They just talked to God like He was their friend. Like He was right there in the room with us.

"So what did you think?" Renee asked as we walked along the lamplit path back to the dorm.

"I liked it," I said.

"Think you'll come back next week?"

"Maybe."

WHERE THERE HAD BEEN NOTHING but empty darkness in my heart, a tiny flame of hope flickered brightly. And suddenly it seemed as if God was showing up everywhere—especially in the lyrics of my favorite songs. The references had been there all along, but now they jumped out at me as though marked by a neon-yellow highlighter.

In "Fire and Rain," James Taylor sang, "Won't you look down upon me, Jesus? You've got to help me make a stand . . ." In "American Pie," Don McLean sang about "the three men I admire the most: The Father, Son and the Holy Ghost." Even raunchy Jethro Tull, in "Locomotive Breath," wailed about how "old Charlie," a self-destructive bloke whose life was careening toward disaster, "picks up a Gideon's Bible, open at page one . . ."

There was also the release of *Jesus Christ Superstar*, Tim Rice and Andrew Lloyd Webber's rock opera, which included an illustrated booklet that told the story of the last week of Christ's life, beginning with Jesus and His followers arriving in Jerusalem and ending with the Crucifixion. You'd think I would have been familiar with the story. But I wasn't, and I found the whole narrative fascinating. When I told Renee, she agreed that Tim Rice and Andrew Lloyd Webber had done a great job, but that they had left out the most important part of the story.

"What's that?" I asked.

"The Resurrection," she said.

After learning about the Resurrection, I was struck by how completely misunderstood Jesus was by those closest to Him. His death on the cross was a scandalous tragedy. His mission on earth an abject failure. When the Resurrection happened, it took everyone—especially those closest to Jesus—by total surprise. It wasn't just a failure of their imagination. It was the ushering in of a whole new reality.

Who could ever imagine that something so beautiful and good—the promise of salvation and eternal life for the whole world—could come out of such a seemingly messy disaster?

If the story was true, when Jesus arrived on earth, it was as though God Himself put skin on and came crashing into human history.

If the story was true.

As I was leaving my journalism class, I bumped into Renee in the hallway.

"You coming tonight?" she asked.

"Okay," I said. I hadn't been to a meeting in a while.

The talk that night was about something called being "born again."

I liked the idea. It captured my imagination. After all, who wouldn't like a chance to start over fresh? *With a fresh start,* I thought, *maybe I can stop secretly stuffing myself with food and throwing up. Maybe that big, aching hole in my heart will finally get filled.*

After the talk, the leader asked if now wouldn't be a good time to "ask Jesus into my heart."

I wasn't exactly sure what it was that I was feeling, but something deep inside of me cried out, *Yes! Yes, I want to believe!*

So on that night, sitting next to Renee, I closed my eyes and prayed.

Dear Jesus, if You're real—and I'm willing to believe that You are—please come into my heart.

THE NEXT MORNING WHEN I AWOKE, I looked out my second-story dormitory window to the campus below. Although it had not rained overnight, the buildings and trees seemed to sparkle and glisten in the dazzling sunlight. The world looked washed clean, fresh and new. Like the way I felt inside.

I reached for the copy of *American Astrology* on my

dresser, to read my daily horoscope, when I had the strangest thought.

You don't need that anymore.

Renee had given me a small paperback version of the New Testament called *Good News for Modern Man*, which I picked up instead. Written in everyday English, it was easy reading.

I opened it, and my eyes fell upon the words of the Apostle Paul in the Book of Romans, who wrote:

"I do not understand what I do; for I don't do what I would like to do, but instead I do what I hate . . . What an unhappy man I am! Who will rescue me from this body that is taking me to death? Thanks be to God, through our Lord Jesus Christ!"

The words filled me with a rush of hope for my battle with anxiety and my secret compulsive bingeing and throwing up. . . .

When suddenly, with breathtaking clarity, I understood what was happening to me. Yesterday my heart had been desolate, dark and empty—utterly devoid of *hope*. Now it was filled to overflowing. God was real. He loved me. It was as simple as that.

"Thank You, God," I whispered.

I didn't know whether to laugh or cry.

Rummaging through my purse, I found a dime and headed out the door, down the hall, past the vending machines to the pay phone. It had been so long since I'd last spoken to my parents, and now I finally had some good news. I was about to drop the dime into the slot, when I stopped.

Not yet, I thought. My relationship with God was too new, too wonderful, too fragile to talk about to anyone. Especially my mother. *What if she doesn't understand? And even if she does, what if she doesn't approve?*

Maybe I would tell her someday.

But not yet.

Amazing Grace

A FEW YEARS AFTER COLLEGE, I took a job as a writer for a magazine in New York City. People say you either love or hate the city. Well, I loved it. Everything about New York energized me—the impatient honk of yellow taxis, the rumble of city buses, the cries of hotdog and pretzel vendors, the bustling sidewalk crowds. There was something about the city that made me feel that something wonderful could happen at any moment—that *anything* was possible.

Through an ad in the *New York Times*, I found an affordable rental in the heart of Greenwich Village on Tenth Street—a cozy second-floor corner apartment with windows that looked out over the green-and-white striped awning of Pierre Deux, the French fabric store on Bleecker Street. My sister lived just a few blocks away, and after work Carolyn and I would meet regularly at Caffe Reggio on MacDougal Street, where we sipped steaming foamy cups of cinnamon-dusted cappuccino and talked about how great it was to be living in the greatest city in the world.

New York was good for my relationship with my

mother too. Over the phone, it was easy to keep our conversations light, simple—and brief. The way my mother liked. The way I liked too.

"You don't want to run up your long-distance phone bill," she would say after a few minutes of chitchat.

"That's true," I'd agree.

"Love you!" she'd chirp, just before hanging up.

"Love you too!" I'd echo.

And that was that.

But as great as it was to be living in the greatest city in the world, I still worried obsessively. And I secretly binged and purged at least once a week—sometimes more.

How is this possible? I wondered. *By now shouldn't God make more of a difference in my life?* I was like the father, so desperate for his son's healing in the Gospel of Mark, who cried, "Lord, I believe. Help my *unbelief*!"

So far, the biggest difference faith had made in my life was that it gave me a persistent *hope* that somehow, someday, I would be healed of my anxiety and set free from my secret problem with food. For now, that hope was enough to keep me going. It was certainly better than nothing.

And although I didn't mention it in any of my phone conversations with my mother, the best thing about New York was that I'd finally discovered a place to call my spiritual home—beautiful Grace Church on the corner of Broadway and Tenth Street.

BUILT IN 1846, Grace Church, with its distinctive lacy spire and beautiful stained glass windows, was an historic downtown landmark, long-recognized as a masterpiece of the Gothic Revival style. But now there was another kind of revival going on. At the eleven o'clock service on Sunday mornings, the pews were crowded with people from all walks of life—young and old, families and single people, graduate students from nearby New York University, attorneys, accountants, advertising and publishing executives, and Wall Street bankers. Because of the church's downtown location, there were also many professional artists, actors, musicians, dancers and writers.

While it was the church's stunning architecture that initially attracted many to step through the carved wooden doors and find a seat in the cool, dimly lit sanctuary, it was the preaching that kept them coming back.

The eleventh Rector of Grace Church was the Reverend Dr. C. FitzSimons Allison—better known as Fitz. Fitz was an academic, a brilliant Oxford educated theologian, author and Professor of Church History at Virginia Theological Seminary. When he arrived at Grace Church, he had little prior experience as a parish priest. But with his soft southern drawl, quick wit and tender heart, he had a winning way with parishioners. Sunday after Sunday, he preached about the amazing power of God's grace to touch and heal the human heart.

Grace, Fitz explained, *was God's unmerited, unearned and unconditional love for every person.* Because of God's grace, he said, Christianity was *not* (contrary to popular opinion) a legalistic, performance-based religion. According to Fitz, there was nothing a person could do—or not do—that would make God love you any more—or any less. This was good news, especially for those struggling to find their way in the highly competitive and materialistic city. Good news, too, for someone like me struggling with anxiety and a shame-inducing secret problem with food.

I started attending a Bible study on Monday nights. And then on Wednesdays after work, I started attending the six o'clock midweek Communion service. After the service, I joined more than two hundred mostly twenty- and thirty-somethings who gathered for a brown bag supper in the church hall, and then split off into prayer groups that met in various offices, apartments, classrooms, hallways, nooks and crannies in the old church. Over time deep friendships were forged. For some, romance blossomed too. There were engagement parties, weddings, baptisms and housewarmings. It was like being part of a great big family.

In order to become an official member of Grace Church, I needed to be confirmed, which was something I'd never done as a child. So I signed up for the six-week course of preparatory classes. On the night before my confirmation, I phoned my mother to tell her about my decision to join the church.

"That's nice," she said, as though I had just told her about a good movie I'd seen. "I'm glad you're going to church. Church is a good place to meet people."

Translation: Church is a good place to meet a *man*.

"Okay, Mom," I said. "I've gotta go."

Why, I wondered, as I hung up the phone, *do I even bother trying to tell her anything?* I felt the old familiar frustration at my inability to connect. *Did she ever feel the same way too?* I wondered. I suddenly felt tired and vaguely anxious. *If only I could stop caring so much about what my mother thinks. I'm not a little girl anymore. Why*, I wondered, *is her approval still so important to me?*

On Confirmation Sunday, I leaned against the pew and gazed at the carved wooden angel in front of the choir stalls. Bent on one knee, with his palms pressed together in prayer, he looked so lifelike that for a moment I thought he might suddenly rise up, spread his feathered wings and take flight. Illuminated by the morning sun, the life-sized figures of the great East Window glowed with deep luminous jewel tones . . . ruby, emerald, sapphire and amethyst. Upheld by the outstretched wings of a majestic brass eagle, a large open Bible rested on the burgundy velvet-wrapped lectern. Permeating the cavernous vaulted sanctuary was the sweet perfume of white stargazer lilies, snowy hydrangeas and creamy roses. For a moment time stood still—it could easily have been one hundred years earlier—until I felt the mosaic-tile floor beneath my feet vibrate with the underground rumbling of a passing subway train.

I turned around just in time to see Carolyn closing the latch on the wooden door of the pew several rows behind me. I raised my hand and waved. She waved back.

In order to ensure a smooth flow during the long service, the Confirmation class sat together as a group. On my right was a handsome dark-haired young man I'd never seen before which was surprising, because I thought by now I was acquainted with just about everybody at Grace Church. Clean-cut, he wore a navy blazer, maroon striped tie, and blue oxford weave button-down collared shirt. Our eyes met.

"Hello," he said, extending his hand. "I'm Tom."

His hand was warm, his grip firm. For a moment I didn't want to let go.

"Nice to meet you," I whispered. "I'm Kitty."

He had the kindest hazel eyes.

The church organ sounded the opening chords of the Processional Hymn and everyone stood. After the sermon it was time for me to leave the pew and find my alphabetical place in the long line of Confirmands.

"Bye," I whispered, touching Tom lightly on the shoulder.

"Good luck," he said. "Nice meeting you. Maybe I'll see you later." His voice was soft and low, and his eyes had a way of twinkling in the most enchanting way. For a second I felt just the tiniest bit light-headed.

"Maybe," I said, trying my best to sound nonchalant.

After all, I told myself, *he's probably already involved with someone else . . .*

Then again, as my mother liked to say, you never know.

The Fire

OUTSIDE MY SECOND-FLOOR apartment window, the black night glowed a hellish red, and a whirlwind of fiery orange sparks turned to ash as they blew against the cold glass. Sirens wailed, and my tiny living room pulsated like a disco dance floor with the flashing red and blue lights of fire trucks.

There was a pounding on the door.

"*Kathryn! Kathryn!*" I recognized the Greek accent of Mr. Thanopoulos, my building superintendent. Wrapping my pink flannel bathrobe tightly around my waist, I unlocked the deadbolt and cracked open the door.

"Kathryn, we need your help. Now. Up on the roof. There's a bad fire one block over, and wind is blowing the sparks. We need everyone in the building to help keep the roof wet, or we'll catch fire too. It is a very dangerous situation."

"Oh dear," I said.

"Kathryn, you *must* come *now*."

"Okay," I said. "I just need time to—to change."

"Very good." Mr. Thanopoulos bounded down the hallway to pound on another door. "But hurry!" he called over his shoulder.

I closed my door and leaned heavily against the wall. My stomach was swollen, hard as a rock. Caught in the middle of a major vanilla fudge twirl ice cream and Entenmann's chocolate chip cookies binge, there was no way I had enough time to finish eating, make myself throw up and pull myself together to join the bucket brigade of tenants on the roof.

When I thought of all the time I had wasted bingeing and purging over the past twelve years—thousands of irreplaceable hours I could have spent building relationships with friends, reading good books, reaching out to help others less fortunate—helping to prevent a fire in my own building, for Pete's sake!—it made me sick. Plus, there was the expense. There was the cost of the food, of course—thousands of dollars literally flushed down the drain. There were also staggering dental bills. At age twenty-eight, the enamel on my teeth had been gradually eaten away by stomach acids, and I had ten porcelain-covered gold crowns. No one, not even the dentist, suspected the reason why.

Is this, I wondered, *what it's like to be an alcoholic? Is it possible that food, like alcohol or drugs, is just another substance capable of being abused?*

My compulsive bingeing was strange in so many ways. Sometimes the temptation slept. But then—like a ravenous roaring lion—it awoke and demanded to be fed. I wasn't entirely helpless. There was always a moment of decision— a particle of a moment—a nanosecond—an infinitesimal flicker—before giving in to the temptation, before surrendering to the urge, before willfully making the damning choice: *Yes, I will binge.* I was not being deceived. I knew exactly that to which I was saying yes. I knew the remorse, guilt and shame that I would feel as a result. But I said yes anyhow.

In the hallway I heard the sound of excited voices, apartment doors slamming and footsteps running up and down the stairs. Outside my window, fiery orange sparks continued to light the night sky. I sat down at the table and dug my spoon into the half-gallon carton of soft, half-melted ice cream. For this moment, only one thing mattered—and that was feeding my insatiable hunger.

I raised the spoon to my open mouth . . .

Fire or no fire, there is no way I'm leaving this apartment. Mr. Thanopoulos and the other tenants will just have to save the building without me.

The binge itself was joyless. A blur. The food could have been anything. That night it was ice cream and cookies, but it could just as easily have been chocolate-covered donuts, scrambled eggs, peanut butter and jam slathered on soft white bread, hot buttered English muffins, still-frozen Sara Lee brownies, whatever was at hand—all washed down by copious amounts of soda, milk, iced tea, water—it didn't matter. All that mattered was that the food was *forbidden*—sweet, rich and comforting. The binge was not so much about eating as it was about *surrendering* to the ravenous, insatiable appetite. And having once surrendered, the prime directive was not to merely eat, but to stuff and gorge. It was obscene. Unnatural. Twisted. And then, when I could eat no more—my belly distended and swollen—there was the *punishment* that waited for giving in to the forbidden food—the consequence for the sin: the God-awful purge.

The purge was so awful, so repulsive, so difficult, so physically painful and exhausting, that I put it off as long as possible. But not too long. I couldn't let the food digest, which would allow the dreaded calories to be absorbed and stored as—*Horrors!*—*fat*.

The procrastinating that preceded the purge was the worst part. It was like being in hell. There I was, physically stuffed, stuck with the food in me, dreading what I was going to have to do to get it out, because the act of making myself throw up was so unnatural, vile, perverse—such a reminder that I was so weak and sick. This was when I was most vulnerable and exposed. This was when I was most afraid. *What if someone phones? Knocks at the door?* When this happened, I sat frozen with fear, and pretended I wasn't there.

But tonight, I'd been caught.

What is it about this secret, sick, compulsive behavior that has such a hold on me? I wondered.

And what if Tom finds out? I shuddered. The thought was terrifying . . .

TOM AND I HAD BEEN DATING for six months. To my great dismay, he had recently moved away from New York to accept a job with a company in Minneapolis, Minnesota. Trying to make the best of the situation, we decided that the separation would be a good test for our relationship. When we said good-bye, we joked that it would be a case of either "absence makes the heart grow fonder," or "out of sight, out of mind." So far, absence was definitely making our hearts grow fonder. We talked on the phone almost every night.

Even so, I thought, *if Tom could see me now—a prisoner in my own apartment—he'd be disgusted. He'd think I was crazy. He'd break up with me for sure . . .*

AS I BENT OVER THE TOILET, my grandmother's silver marcasite cross dangled over the bowl, mocking me.

And you call yourself a Christian? How can you be a Christian and be so weak? How can you be a Christian and do this awful thing over and over and over? God sees what you're doing. He knows the truth. You're nothing but a fraud!

I flipped the cross behind my neck, pulled back my hair, and stuck two fingers down my throat—not just once, but two . . . three . . . four . . . five . . . six . . . seven . . . eight times . . . then again . . . and again . . . until there was nothing left to come up from my stomach but bitter yellow bile.

After the purge, there was the initial relief that the food was gone, but my throat was raw, and I was exhausted. My head swirled with a dark whirlpool of guilt, shame and self-loathing—emotionally crippling feelings I couldn't get rid of so easily as the food—feelings that would poison my dreams and, when I awoke, feelings that would poison my relationships with others. Because if anyone knew the *truth* about what I did—how weak and sick I really was— they would so utterly, completely, and—let's face it— *justifiably* reject me.

"Dear Father," I cried out in despair, as I staggered from the bathroom, "please help me. Oh, Daddy, please help me."

'Daddy?' I thought. *Did I actually say that? What was that about? Oh, God, I must really be losing it.*

SOMETIME AFTER MIDNIGHT when the threat of the fire had passed, and I had finished bingeing and purging, I crawled into bed. Exhausted and filled with remorse for my behavior, I opened my Bible and came across this promise: "I will restore to you the years which the swarming locust has eaten . . ."

Is it really possible, I wondered, *for God to somehow restore the years I have lost, helplessly enslaved to food?* Possible—yes. Jesus said that with God all things were possible.

But the way things were going, not likely.

Off the Pedestal

A FEW WEEKS LATER, my parents came to the city to visit. It was my father's birthday, and we met at a neighborhood bistro to celebrate. Though truth be told, there wasn't much to celebrate . . .

MY FATHER'S CAREER was over. Six years before, at the age of fifty-six, with failing health, he had reluctantly agreed to take early retirement. What really hurt was that he had ignominiously been replaced by a younger executive whom he had hired. "The one mistake I made," he said, in a rare reflective moment, "was that I didn't set my career goals high enough."

Oh, Dad, I thought sadly. *Why can't you see that your problem is alcohol?* But who was I to criticize, considering my problem with food?

My parents sold our house in Miami and moved to Palm Harbor, a small town on Florida's west coast, near my mother's parents' winter home. My father tried working as a real-estate agent, spending Saturday and Sunday afternoons sitting at open houses, but he soon lost interest. He talked a lot about going fishing, but never seemed to have the energy to do it. "Too much trouble," he said. And he continued drinking . . . a lot.

NOW MY FATHER'S THINNING HAIR and moustache were silver-gray, and when he put on his black horn-rimmed glasses to read the menu, they seemed too large for his face. He looked like an old man—certainly much older than his sixty-two years.

After paying the bill, we decided to walk the five-block distance home to my apartment. It was a beautiful December night. The air was crisp and clear. High overhead, a full moon shone on the bare branches of the ginkgo trees lining Tenth Street, casting lacy shadows on the sidewalk.

Several times along the way, my father had to stop and catch his breath.

"You go on ahead," he said, sitting on the cold granite steps leading up to a red brick brownstone. He waved his hand. "Go. I'll be fine."

"No way," I said. "We can wait."

It took us nearly an hour to get home. In my apartment, he steadied himself against the kitchen counter.

"Dad?" I asked. "What's wrong?"

"Sorry, Scooter," he said. "I'm not feeling so well."

His face was gaunt. His hands were trembling and his belly appeared swollen.

My God, I thought. *He's dying.*

"Mom?" I turned to face my mother, who was filling a glass of water for him at the kitchen sink. "What's going on?"

"Your dad is sick," she said. "The doctors say there's something wrong with his liver."

"Don't worry," he snapped. "It's nothing." He sighed wearily. "I'll be fine. I'm just tired, that's all. I think— I think it's time we all said good night."

So we did.

AT WORK, part of my job was looking for new story ideas. A few days after my parents' visit, I was sitting at my desk, thumbing through the latest issue of *People* magazine, when my eyes froze on a bold headline about a "New Dangerous Binge/Purge Cycle" that caused women to overeat compulsively and then, in a desperate effort to get rid of the calories, "purge by means of self-induced vomiting." Women who binged and purged, the article said, had a poor body image. Perfectionists, they also tended to suffer extreme anxiety. As a result of their uncontrollable bingeing and purging they often felt "shame, loneliness, isolation, guilt and terror at being found out."

I could hardly believe what I was reading.

The new binge/purge cycle was called *bulimia nervosa.*

The Latin word *bulimia* means "extreme hunger." Bulimia, like the newly identified anorexia nervosa, was something psychiatrists called an "eating disorder." According to the article, at least four percent of American females would suffer bulimia at some point in their lifetime.

A sense of relief washed over me, and I started to cry.

I'm not alone! Moreover, I wasn't crazy. I was sick. I was "disordered." *Disordered.* How perfectly the word captured the twisted, unnatural, tyrannical, and emotional push-and-pull of the disease.

After so many years of keeping my terrible secret, I wanted to tell my mother. Although I dreaded it. And Tom— I would have to tell him too. I dreaded that even more.

I closed my office door, sat down at my desk, and nervously pushed the buttons on the phone.

My mother picked up right away. She had just returned home from taking my father to the doctor. In a rush of words, I told her about the article, and how I was so sorry to have to tell her that I had this thing called bulimia, and that I wasn't crazy, just sick, and that I would send her a copy of the article.

There was a long silence.

She cleared her throat.

"Well, whatever it is you're dealing with, *I* certainly had nothing to do with it," she said. Silence again. And then, "You're *not going to tell Tom*, are you?"

Translation: You'd better not tell him, or he'll drop you for sure.

"No, no—that's not why I called," I said. "I just—I just wanted to tell you. I mean, I thought you should know. I'm sorry. I really am."

Blinking back tears, I hung up the phone.

Stupid me! What was I thinking? After all these years, why did I ever think she would suddenly understand? And why did I feel I had to tell her anyhow? I am an adult. I can take care of myself.

Now when I look back, I can see that my mother probably had a lot on her mind, taking care of my father. But oh, if only she could have said something like, "I'm so sorry." Or, "Oh, honey, I knew there was something wrong with you—but I could never figure out what it was." Or, "It doesn't matter. I still love you." But she hadn't.

That night, back in my apartment, it was Tom's turn to call me from Minneapolis.

At 9:00 PM, I fixed myself a cup of herbal tea and sat waiting by the phone, clutching the magazine. After my experience with my mother, I dreaded telling Tom about my problem with food. But I knew it was something I had to do—even though it would likely mean the end of our relationship.

The phone rang, and I jumped.

"Tom?"

"What's wrong, Kitty?" he asked. "You don't sound like yourself."

"There's something I have to tell you," I said. And for the second time that day, in a torrent of tears and words I confessed my deepest, darkest shame-filled secret.

There was a long silence.

"Kitty?"

"Yes?" My heart pounded with fear, and I closed my eyes, waiting to hear the worst.

"You know," Tom said quietly, "I never had you on a pedestal."

"What—what do you mean?"

"I mean, I never expected you to be perfect. I guess what I'm trying to say is—I love you."

"You do?"

"Don't worry," Tom said softly. I could almost see his tender smile. "The fact you're talking about your problem is the first step toward getting better. We'll work through this thing together."

"Oh, Tom," I whispered. "*Thank you.*"

The fact that Tom accepted and loved me despite my weaknesses and shortcomings—with full knowledge of my tendency toward anxiety and my problem with food—was profoundly and powerfully healing. Getting better wouldn't happen overnight. It would take time. But now at least I had someone to talk to. Someone to pray with.

Someone to walk alongside me—if only through long-distance phone calls—encouraging me along the way.

A FEW DAYS LATER, I was walking home from church along Tenth Street. Now, in the harsh and unforgiving midday sun, the ginkgo trees didn't look pretty at all. They looked naked and dead. I thought of my father and felt overwhelmed with sadness.

The sermon that Sunday had been about how Jesus' relationship was so close to His heavenly Father that when He prayed, He used the word "*Abba*," which in His native Aramaic language literally meant "Daddy." Apparently this caused quite an uproar among the religious leaders of the day. To suggest that anyone could relate to the God of the Universe, the great Creator of all humankind, with such *unabashed intimacy* was nothing short of scandalous.

I remembered the night of the neighborhood fire when in despair I had cried out to "Daddy" in prayer. At the time, I had thought that it was an inadvertent slip of the tongue.

Now I wondered.

My earthly father was dying. Was it possible that through my *faith* I could crawl onto my heavenly Father's lap and rest my head on His strong chest? That I could feel the warmth of His acceptance and love, and actually hear Him say, "*This is my beloved daughter with whom I am well pleased?*"

I was beginning to believe it was.

No Time for Small Talk

W HEN MY FATHER got so sick he had to be admitted to the hospital, Carolyn and I flew down to Florida to spend the weekend with my mother, who was pretty worn out.

It had been five months since I'd last seen my father, back when we celebrated his birthday in the city. His decline was shocking. Emaciated and jaundiced, he looked like an old, old man. It was hard for me to look at him without crying. We stood around his hospital bed making mostly small talk. He asked if I would scratch his back, and so I did—but not too hard. He was nothing but skin and bones.

After our visit, we met with the doctor who told us he couldn't say for sure how long my father would live. Maybe a few months. But not much longer. His case of advanced alcoholic cirrhosis, or scarring of the liver, was fatal. Back then, there was no such thing as a liver transplant.

That evening after dinner, my mother and sister turned on the television to watch the NBC Saturday night movie. I had just closed the latch on the dishwasher and pressed the start button when I had the strangest thought.

Go back to the hospital.

I untied my apron and hung it on the magnetic hook attached to the refrigerator.

Just my imagination, I thought. *It's been a long day.* But there it was again. This time, insistent.

Go back to the hospital. Now!

I grabbed a sweater, fished the car keys out of the dish by the front door, and headed for the garage. I didn't tell my mother and sister that I was leaving. If I did, they would surely ask why, and I was afraid I didn't have much of an answer.

OUTSIDE MY FATHER'S HOSPITAL ROOM a meal cart was parked with dirty dinner dishes. The door was slightly ajar.

"Dad?"

His eyes were closed, and with great difficulty he turned his head toward the sound of my voice. I pulled a green plastic chair close to his bedside.

"Hey, Dad, it's me."

He slowly opened his eyes. The whites were bleary and yellow with jaundice, but the irises were still a startling bright blue. He opened his mouth slightly, as if to speak, but no words came out.

"Dad, I just want to let you know that I love you," I reached for his hand and held it tightly. "I've always loved you. You're the most wonderful father anyone could ever have, and I'm—I'm so sorry for anything I ever said or did that might have caused you to think otherwise." The words and tears came spilling out from some deep, untapped reservoir in my soul. There was such a sense of urgency. Time was short. This was my last chance to get through to my father.

This was no time for small talk.

"I love you so much," I spoke softly in his ear. "And God does too. And someday you'll be in heaven, and your sister Mary Louise will be there too—she's already there waiting for you. And everything will be beautiful and wonderful and good . . ."

A tiny smile played at the corner of his parched lips.

"Great," he whispered. I felt his fingers relax. And then he closed his eyes.

A nurse appeared in the doorway.

"Visiting hours are over," she frowned. "Is everything all right here?"

I nodded. "I'll be leaving soon," I said. "I promise." I waited until the squishy sound of her white rubber-soled shoes disappeared down the long hallway.

"Dad?"

His eyes remained closed, and his chest moved up and down slowly. He was sleeping peacefully.

"Good-bye, Dad." I kissed his forehead lightly. "I love you."

WHEN I GOT BACK TO THE HOUSE, my mother and sister were still in front of the television, right where I'd left them. Thankfully, they hadn't even missed me.

I hung up my sweater, and returned the car keys to the dish by the door. As I settled on the sofa next to Carolyn, I absentmindedly touched the smooth gold band that circled my left ring finger. My engagement ring. For a brief moment my sadness lifted, and my heart fluttered with joy . . .

I STILL COULDN'T BELIEVE that Tom had asked me to marry him. Getting married had never been part of my plan. Not that I could say for sure what my "plan" had been—oh, something about living in New York . . . getting a good job . . . traveling . . . maybe even falling in love someday. But getting married?

Not in my wildest dreams.

Off the Chart

B ECAUSE OF THE UNCERTAINTY associated with my father's illness and impending death, Tom and I decided to get married as simply and quickly as possible. Minneapolis would be the location, since that's where we would be living. No one from my family would be able to attend. But that was all right. Just as I had never planned on getting married, I'd never dreamed of a big fancy wedding, either.

In the days leading up to the wedding, there was a part of me that was nervous about moving so far away, where the only person I knew was Tom—whom I'd known for less than a year. Let's face it. There was a part of me that was nervous about getting married.

What will it be like living day-in, day-out with someone? I worried. *What if my anxiety flares up in some unexpected, unpleasant way? Worse yet, what if my bulimia, which is barely under control, comes roaring back?*

HAPPILY, THE WEDDING WENT OFF without a hitch. Tom's family was able to join us, and his older brother Jim kindly offered to stand in for my father to walk me down the aisle and "give me away."

We were married just eight days when my mother telephoned with the sad news that my father had died. We flew together to Florida for the funeral, after which Tom flew back to Minneapolis, and I returned to New York to tie up loose ends at work and close up my apartment.

NOW, AS I SAT ON THE FLOOR wrapping my books and typewriter in old newspapers and packing them in a brown cardboard box, it occurred to me that my father had actually died a long time ago. That is, the sense of *losing* him had been present for as many years as he had been drinking. Even so, waves of grief continued to take me by surprise, crashing against my heart with unexpected force and intensity.

I sealed the box shut with packing tape and labeled it with a black felt tip marker: OFFICE. In Minnesota, I would continue working from our basement, where Tom had fashioned a large desktop made from a wooden door balanced on two sawhorses.

Grunting, I lifted the box and carried it to the hallway, where I dropped it onto the mountain of other boxes stacked for the movers. Wiping my hands on my jeans, I wondered briefly how my mother was holding up.

But only briefly.

A few months earlier I'd signed a contract with a publisher for a collaborative memoir with the current Miss America. Then I got another book contract, this time for a collaboration with a psychiatrist at Duke University.

When I told my mother over the phone about the new assignments, she said, "Oh, Kitty, that's great! *Now* you'll *really* be in the big time!" But what I heard then was, *"Everything you've done up until now has been nothing but peanuts."*

Maybe I was being supersensitive.

Maybe not.

AFTER SO MANY YEARS LIVING ALONE with bulimia, my biggest adjustment to married life concerned how I shopped for, prepared, and—most significantly—consumed food. Now, on trips to the grocery store, I avoided purchasing favorite binge foods, like packaged cookies, cakes, ice cream and brownies. At home in our new apartment, Tom and I shared almost every meal together. And in the late evening—during those dangerous hours when I might be most tempted to binge—I was no longer alone. Bingeing was a solitary activity. Purging was lengthy and noisy. Even if I had wanted to give in to the bulimic binge-purge urge, our apartment was too small for me to get away with it.

WE'D BEEN MARRIED for about a month, when one morning I surprised Tom with buttermilk pancakes for breakfast. After breakfast, he kissed me good-bye and headed off to work.

"Have a good day!" he called over his shoulder as he headed down the stairs.

"You too!" I said.

At the sound of the garage door closing, I felt a sudden, unexpected pang of loneliness. I missed New York. My old church. My old friends. The camaraderie of my old office. I didn't want to go to work all alone at my sawhorse desk in the basement.

How can this be? I thought. *I love Tom. With all my heart. We are happy . . . aren't we?*

I carried the breakfast dishes to the sink. On the serving platter was a stack of uneaten pancakes. Still warm. I inhaled their fragrant yeasty aroma. I sliced a soft pat of butter and spread it across the top pancake and watched it dissolve. I sliced another pat, and then another, inserting pat after pat between each layer until the whole stick of butter was gone. On automatic pilot, I reached for the bottle of maple syrup and poured it over the stack of pancakes, watching it dribble down the sides and collect on the platter into a sweet sticky pool. I picked up a fork . . .

Just one bite, I thought. *Just one . . .*

But before the thought was formed, I knew it would never be "just one bite." I was in full-binge mode. When the stack of pancakes had disappeared, I unwrapped a loaf of whole wheat bread and slathered one slice after another with peanut butter and grape jelly . . . I ate and ate and ate, until I could eat no more. Then I went into the bathroom—*our* bathroom—and made myself throw up.

And then I cried.

I felt terrible. I hated myself. I felt as though I had defiled our new apartment.

Worse, I felt as though I had defiled our *marriage*.

That night, when Tom came home, I told him what I'd done. I said I was sorry, and that I would try—really try—to never do it again.

"Don't worry," he said, shaking his head. "You've had this problem a long time. It's not going to disappear overnight. Look back over the past several months. You've made a lot of progress. You've just got to keep on being honest about it—like you're doing." He hugged me tightly. "Look on the bright side. You're doing better than you think."

A few more weeks passed without bingeing, and then—after being married just two months—I got pregnant.

The fact that I was expecting further steeled my resolve to eat healthily. It wasn't just about me anymore. There was another human life at stake. I didn't mind my expanding belly one bit. The bigger the better. And the first time I felt the baby move, I shivered with wonder and delight.

As months passed, more information became available

about bulimia. I learned that it is a much more common eating disorder than anorexia nervosa. I was among the estimated four percent of women, and ten percent of college-age women, who would suffer bulimia in their lifetime. But many experts claimed that even these percentages grossly underestimated the problem, because so many bulimics are able to hide their purging and do not become noticeably underweight. Bulimia, I learned, is primarily a women's disorder, but men can suffer from it too. In addition to self-induced vomiting, some bulimics purge by taking laxatives and using enemas, severe dieting, excessive exercise, and by abusing over-the-counter appetite suppressants, diuretics and vomit-inducing drugs such as Ipecac.

Most importantly, I learned that bulimic bingeing is typically triggered by *confusing hunger with other real feelings*—in my case, episodes of acute anxiety, insecurity, grief, anger, loneliness, and sadness. Other feelings that can be mistaken for hunger include stress, depression, guilt, shame, disgust, jealousy, irritation, shyness, impatience, frustration—even boredom, fatigue and exhaustion. To abuse food in order to relieve negative feelings may, in the short term, "work." But in the long term, the food-abuser remains stuck with the original negative feelings, *plus* enslaved to the compulsive behavior pattern. This is more than a "food problem" or "bad eating habit." This is a life-destroying compulsion, potentially as deadly as any full-blown addiction.

Even though I was married, there would be times when I would find myself alone and tempted. But with each passing day and Tom's support, the urge to binge and purge was gradually fading. I still battled anxiety, but the ravenous roaring lion that was bulimia was finally leaving me alone. Oh, the *temptation* to binge compulsively was occasionally still there, but not as strong.

I began to understand how difficult it would be to get completely well. Even with insight into the root causes of my illness, given the right emotional trigger, the temptation to binge could surface at any time. I held on firmly to the belief that the day would come when I would be fully healed. At the same time, I acknowledged that for the rest of my life I would always be—like an alcoholic—a "recovering" bulimic.

Still, I was so much better than I used to be.

WHEN I WAS EIGHT MONTHS PREGNANT, my mother's mother died. But because I was so far along in my pregnancy, I wasn't able to join Mom and Carolyn for the funeral in Niagara Falls. Sitting in church with Tom, I felt the old familiar tug of family. It was Mother's Day Sunday and I felt guilty—as though by not attending the funeral I was failing to meet a family obligation.

In the past thirteen months I had lost my father and now, both of my grandparents. I'd also gotten married, moved halfway across the country, taken on a new writing project, and was about to become a mother. "Are you stressed?" a recent magazine article asked. "Take this quiz and find out." I took the quiz. And failed miserably. According to the editors, my stress-level score was "Off the Chart—You May Need Help!"

As the minister led us in the Lord's Prayer, I remembered how when I first moved to Minneapolis, I had missed my old life in New York. But now I was beginning to see how it was good for me to be separated from everything old and familiar. Being away from the push and pull of my entrenched family dynamics helped me bond more strongly and closely to my husband. When I felt the onset of anxiety, Tom's common sense level-headedness offered a reality check against my irrational fears. When I was tempted to binge, I admitted it. Not only to Tom—but to God too. Sometimes we prayed together, thanking God for bringing us into each other's lives, and asking for His day-to-day help and guidance.

I remembered how when we got married, the minister had referred to marriage as something called a *sacrament*, which he said was "an outward visible sign of an inner invisible spiritual reality." Back then I had no idea what he was talking about. But now I was beginning to understand. In a very real way, God was somehow tenderly working *through my husband* to heal me. Sometimes I felt so overwhelmed with gratitude for this totally undeserved expression of God's grace—for the *gift* of this patient, loving man—that it made me cry . . .

Sighing, I settled back against the pew. I rested my hand on my huge stomach. The baby was kicking like a little prize fighter. Tom placed his hand over mine and smiled. Our baby was due in six weeks. After so much sadness and loss, I could hardly wait.

My father was gone. My mother was far away.

Tom and I were on our own.

As we stood for the closing hymn, I remembered how in the days leading up to our marriage I had worried so about what it would be like living day-in, day-out with my new husband. It turned out that getting married was the best thing that could have ever happened.

When, I wondered, *will I ever learn to stop worrying?*

A Different Kind of Love

WHEN TOM AND I phoned my mother with the happy news of our daughter Katy's birth, she insisted on flying out to Minneapolis right away.

"Are you sure?" I asked.

"You're going to need a lot of help," she said.

"Okay." I reluctantly agreed.

During my mother's five-day visit, she commandeered the telephone and told everyone who called that I was "resting"—even when I wasn't. She said that phone calls and too many visitors would tire me out. That's what had happened, she said, when I was born. She bought bags and bags of groceries and prepared a month's supply of casseroles that she wrapped in aluminum foil and carefully labeled with her elegant curlicue "Palmer Method" penmanship—*Jones Sausage Casserole . . . Buttonwood Casserole . . . Tuna Puff Casserole . . .* before pushing them into the crowded freezer. She *oohed* and *aahed* at baby gifts the postman delivered—pink hand-knitted booties, a miniature pair of rosebud print OshKosh B'Gosh overalls, and a fuzzy, pastel menagerie of stuffed ducks, turtles, frogs and teddy bears.

And when she picked up her new granddaughter, her eyes shone in a way I'd never seen before. At least not that I could remember.

"Such a *good* little girl," she cooed.

After my mother returned to her home in Florida, and I was alone holding my new daughter, I heard myself cooing the exact same words with the exact same intonation.

"Such a *good* little girl . . ."

There were nursery rhymes, too, that seemed to materialize from out of nowhere.

"Ride a cock-horse to Bunbury Cross," I bounced Katy on my knee and chanted in a new, yet oddly familiar sing songy voice. " . . .To see a fine lady upon a white horse. With rings on her fingers, and bells on her toes . . . She shall have music wherever she goes!"

Where in the world did that come from? I wondered.

It was as though the words and songs, like seeds, had been planted long ago. And now, as naturally and miraculously as the warm sun on a gentle spring day, my baby daughter was coaxing them to emerge like tender green shoots out of the darkness . . .

WEEKS LATER, Katy was cradled in my left arm, napping. She looked like a plump, furled flower bud. But on this particular summer afternoon, with every heat and humidity record being broken, I felt no rosy raptures of motherhood. Hot, tired, crabby and frustrated was more like it.

Earlier in the day, my mother had phoned and asked, "So how's the baby? Is everything under control?"

Under control? I thought.

The day before, my goal had been ridiculously simple: to make tuna salad. Early in the morning I had set out the necessary ingredients and utensils: two cans of tuna fish, a bunch of celery, a jar of mayonnaise, salt, pepper, a stainless steel mixing bowl, a can opener and a spoon. Now, twenty-four hours later, they were all still sitting there on the kitchen counter, untouched.

Under control?

"Yeah, Mom." I capitulated, eager to end the conversation. "Everything's under control. The baby's doing fine."

"Great!" she said. "That's all I wanted to hear."

I hung up the phone, grateful that my daughter was doing fine. But as for me—I wasn't so sure. For the first eight weeks of Katy's life, my life had been reduced to a monotonous round of changing diapers, waking three times a night for feedings, soothing her cries—and worrying.

How could I know for sure what my daughter's cries meant? Was she hungry? Lonely? Sick? Or just uncomfortable from the heat?

The new car seat, stroller, and baby swing had all come with pages of instructions. If only my new baby did too!

Now, after twenty minutes of fussing, Katy had finally drifted off in the crook of my arm. I sat at the dining room table, my free right hand busily scribbling the first of scores of long overdue thank-you notes. An unfamiliar noise caused me to look up.

Cruncha-cruncha-cruncha.

Across the room our calico cat Indy nibbled at the leaves of my one healthy potted plant.

How I wanted to yell a loud, outraged "*Shoo!*" How I ached to jump up off my chair and chase the cat. But to do so would wake my sleeping baby. I was stuck. Trapped. Frustrated beyond belief, my fingers closed around the ball point pen in my hand and I flung it toward the cat. It hit the wall above the plant and clattered to the floor. Regarding me coolly, Indy continued to nibble the green leaves.

Ashamed, I sat very still and squeezed my eyes shut. Warm drops ran into the corners of my mouth and I took a shaky breath.

Oh, God, I prayed silently. *That wasn't very grown-up of me, was it? Sometimes being a mother makes me feel overwhelmed. Helpless.*

I leaned back in the chair and studied my baby girl. This tiny fragile bud of a human being. My daughter. I remembered so clearly the feeling that came over me the night Tom and I brought Katy home from the hospital. Together we leaned on the rail of her crib and watched her sleeping soundly in her new home for the first time. I looked at that sweet face, the perfectly modeled fingers and toes, the petite upturned nose, and felt millions of tiny dancing bubbles well up inside of me—a different kind of love. Not like my love for Tom. Or my father. Or my mother. Or my sister. This love was newborn, like my baby. Unlike anything I'd ever felt before, it filled me with a fierce tenderness. I would do anything to protect this tiny creature, so dependent on me for her life.

The memory was good. Like a gentle hand taking mine. And as I looked down on my sleeping daughter, a new thought dawned.

Without You, God, I'm as helpless and dependent as my child. But You take care of me, giving me the strength to take care of her.

WEEKS PASSED. It was late in the summer now, and the heat wave had broken. I was in the basement loading clothes into the dryer. Katy was upstairs asleep in her crib. Suddenly I heard her cry. There was an anguished note to it, as though she felt utterly abandoned. I slammed the dryer door shut, dashed up the stairs and wrapped her in my arms.

"There, there," I crooned, holding her close to my breast, the soft curve of her head nesting perfectly in the hollow under my chin. "Please don't cry. Mommy's here. Mommy's always here. I'll never leave you, my little Katy."

I couldn't remember ever having called my mother "Mommy." It was somehow too intimate and endearing. It was somehow too sweet. Katy and I settled into the bentwood rocker and relaxed in its soothing rhythm. *Back and forth . . . back and forth . . . back and forth . . .* until, like a gentle breeze, the words came to me—God's promise to *His* children: "Lo, I am with you always."

Dear God, I thought, *You always hear me when I cry too. You are always there, aren't You?*

THE LONG MINNESOTA WINTER PASSED, and Katy was beginning to walk. Sitting cross-legged on the grassy lawn, I watched my intrepid explorer start up the steps leading to the wooden deck at the back of the apartment. At the base of the steps was a slab of poured concrete. Poised on the first step, Katy turned to face me, her eyes shining with pride in her accomplishment. But her legs, unsteady, began to wobble.

Even before I moved to catch her, I knew I was too late. Down she went, face-first, whacking her forehead on the concrete.

"*Katy!*"

Her brow was scraped and bleeding, already purple with an ugly bruise. She was screaming, and as I picked her up, nightmarish fears darkened my mind. *Concussion . . . skull fracture . . . brain damage . . .*

Still carrying her, I raced up the steps and into our bedroom where the well-worn copy of Dr. Spock's *Baby and Child Care* rested on my bedside table. As I scanned the book's pages about head injuries, her cries seemed to subside. According to Dr. Spock, she was showing no symptoms of having suffered anything serious. I sponged her forehead with a cool washcloth, and then held her on my lap murmuring words of love. Minutes later she was all smiles, playing with the cat as though nothing had happened.

But I was still shaken.

Oh, God, I thought, *I feel my daughter's pain so deeply. Is it possible that this is how You love me too?*

IT WAS A BRILLIANT SUMMER DAY and little nuisances had stolen the morning. Within the hour, Tom was expecting us to meet him for lunch at his office in downtown Minneapolis. But I was still in my nightgown. And so was Katy. Seated in her high chair, she had more egg in her hair and on her cheeks than in her tummy, and she was blissfully oblivious to our need to hurry.

Across the room the television was tuned to *Sesame Street.* A big blue letter "K" danced across the screen. Katy caught sight of it and threw her hands skyward—inadvertently launching a full mug of milk across the dining room.

"*Katy!*—"

I was about to scold, when I caught myself. In recent days I'd noticed how sensitive my daughter seemed to my moods and reprimands, especially when my tone was harsh.

She regarded me warily.

"Katy," I repeated calmly, bending over to pick up the empty mug. "Do you know what you say when you spill your milk?" I touched her tousled head and smiled. "You say, '*Oops!*'"

A big sunny grin lit her face, and I wiped up the floor feeling so grateful for not giving in to irritation.

Thank You, God, I thought. *You are forever patient. Even in my worst moments, you still love me. You always offer forgiveness.*

I looked in wonder at the little figure in the high chair. My daughter. Although she couldn't know it, she was creating a new love in me. Mother love. Fresh from heaven, she was also surprising me with glimpses of God's love— the perfect love of my heavenly *Abba Father*—eternally caring, patient and forgiving.

Thank You, God, for my daughter!

And then I had a peculiar thought.

Is it possible that this was how my mother once felt about me too?

Not Your Grandma's Grandma

AFTER TWO YEARS in Minnesota, Tom took a position with a firm in New York. I was thrilled to be back in the city. Once again we were living downtown in our old familiar Greenwich Village neighborhood. Tom took the subway to his job in midtown Manhattan, and I divided my time between being a mom to our daughter Katy and working from an office in our bedroom. I also became pregnant with our second child.

It was around this time that my mother decided something rather remarkable: She thought it might be fun to move to New York too. At age sixty-seven, she said she was tired of living in a part of Florida where there were so many elderly people and so much sickness and death—"the land of the newly-wed and nearly-dead," was the way she put it. In New York, she said, she could be close to her two daughters and grandchildren. She could begin a new chapter in her life.

"Maybe you should try it out first," suggested Carolyn. "Just to be sure."

So when a summer sublet became available in my sister's building, my mother took it. She liked it so much that she sold her house in Florida and bought a handsome two-bedroom penthouse apartment near Grace Church, just a short walk away from my sister and me.

One afternoon, when Carolyn and I were helping Mom hang pictures in her new apartment, she told us that her neighbors back in Florida had said she was *crazy* to move to New York.

"I'm not, am I?" she asked. It was a rhetorical question.

"You just wait, Mom," Carolyn grinned. "You're going to have the time of your life here in New York. If I know you, before long, you'll be leaving the rest of us in the dust!"

My sister was right.

My mother took to life in the big city as though she had lived there forever. She quickly made new friends and handily learned the city bus routes. She spent her days hosting luncheons and teas, catching Wednesday matinees on Broadway, attending openings at the Metropolitan Museum of Art and—her favorite pastime—shopping for bargains at Macy's, Bloomingdale's, and Lord & Taylor.

Sometimes I had to laugh. Our lives couldn't be more different. As a young mother with a baby on the way, I spent my days pushing a heavily laden stroller along cracked city sidewalks, shopping at neighborhood grocery stores for bargains on baby food and disposable diapers.

I was grateful that my sister lived close by. Carolyn's

relationship with Mom was not so prickly as mine. They enjoyed shopping together. If anything, they were more like friends. Best friends. Sometimes I envied their closeness.

One day the phone rang.

"*Oh!*" my mother exclaimed, upon hearing my voice. "I'm sorry, Kitty. I meant to call Carolyn, but must have dialed your number by mistake. Anyhow, Eleanor Bradford just phoned from Niagara. Her daughter had twins! You remember the Bradfords, don't you? They lived two doors down from us on McKinley Avenue?"

"No, Mom," I said. "I don't remember. We moved away from Niagara Falls when I was a baby."

"Of course," my mother said. "What was I thinking?"

Both my sister and mother thought of Niagara Falls as their hometown. Sometimes when they got to talking about old friends and neighbors, I felt a little left out. Ten years between siblings can be a big gap. Indeed, there were times when I felt like Carolyn and I grew up in two different families.

MY MOTHER WAS A STRONG WOMAN—proud and fiercely independent. When she looked to the future, there were only two things she feared: losing her vision, and someday winding up an unwilling resident in a nursing home.

Her fears were not unreasonable. My mother's eyesight had always been poor. She'd worn glasses since childhood, and her father had lost his vision to age-related macular degeneration, so that by the time he was in his early eighties he was declared legally blind. After he died, Mom's mother, who suffered senile dementia, was unable to live alone and spent the last year of her life in the nursing home wing of a Niagara Falls hospital. Sometimes, my mother said, she worried about these two things so much that she couldn't sleep.

One morning I stopped by her apartment unexpectedly. When she answered the door, her eyes were red-rimmed and puffy.

"What's wrong with your eyes?" I asked.

"Oh, they're just tired," she said. "I didn't get much sleep last night." She sniffed, and dabbed her nose with a hankie.

"Mom," I asked, "have you been *crying*?"

"Oh, Kitty," she sobbed, slumping onto the sofa. "I feel so bad that I wasn't there for her."

"There for *who*?" I asked.

"My mother," she said. "I wasn't there for her when she needed me. She hated that nursing home. I just know she did."

"But you lived so far away," I said. "She was all the way up in Niagara Falls, and you were down in Florida. Plus, you had so much going on in your life. You were taking care of Dad, remember? And then he *died*. You did the best you could. Surely your mother understood. You know she loved you so much."

But Mom just shook her head.

"I should have been there," she said. "I'm her daughter, and I should have been there when she needed me most."

WITH THE ARRIVAL OF OUR SON, my mother became the proud grandmother of two. She loved our children Katy and Brinck, and welcomed their visits to her apartment. She rejoiced in their accomplishments, lavished them with gifts, and even treated them to a trip to Disney World. But in many ways she was not your typical grandmother. The kids did not call her "Grandma" or "Nana" or "Grammy." They called her "Mama B." (for Brinckerhoff). She would not be a babysitter, she made that clear. Her mother had not babysat for her grandchildren, she said, nor would she. So her phone number appeared at the bottom of my list of sitters, under the category "In Case of Emergency."

My mother refused to get "old." She was thin and stylish as ever, without a trace of gray in her auburn hair. Should anyone make the mistake of asking her age, she laughed her lilting ice-cube laugh and said she was "thirty-nine and holding." She was sophisticated. A world traveler. Up on current events. She was definitely "with it."

I admired and respected all these things about my mother. But every once in a while I found myself wishing that she could be a little bit more—grandmotherly. A little bit more white-haired, soft and pillowy.

AT LEAST NOW MY MOTHER and I finally had something in common: We both loved New York. At the same time, every once in a while I felt like she was intruding on my turf. New York had been *my* city, Greenwich Village *my* neighborhood, Grace Church *my* church. Now I had to share all these things with her too? *Shame on you*, I scolded myself. *The city belongs to millions. It's certainly big enough for both of us.*

Then one day I watched as my mother took a photograph of the kids with her Kodak Instamatic. Squatting down low, she held the camera vertically and bobbed back and forth.

Who does she think she is? I wondered. *Margaret Bourke-White? Annie Leibovitz?* She was using a totally automatic camera, for Pete's sake. All she had to do was point and shoot. With a start, I realized she was unconsciously imitating the way *I* took pictures with my all-manual 35mm single-lens reflex camera.

Then there was the Sunday morning I stood in the church hall during social hour, balancing a coffee cup in one hand, while holding onto my wiggly toddler son with the other. Suddenly I felt a finger run down my spine.

"*Posture!*" I heard my mother's voice whisper in my ear. "You don't want to slouch."

Recoiling from her touch, I moved a few steps away. Like I was thirteen years old.

Another time I was visiting my mother at her apartment when the phone rang.

"Yes," I heard her say, "I'm so glad *we* made the decision to move to New York. *We're* just loving it."

"*We?*" I wondered. *It's been years since Dad died. Does she mean Carolyn and me? Or perhaps she is using the "royal 'we'"* . . .

And suddenly I felt an unexpected pang of sympathy. Even with her busy life and being surrounded by family, it must be so *lonely* to be a widow. She and my father, despite his alcoholism, had a strong marriage and loved each other very much. Plus, I'd noticed that whenever anyone asked my mother how her husband had died, she said it was from cancer, not cirrhosis of the liver. She said it so easily, and with such conviction, I think that's what she really believed.

As TIME PASSED, I still battled with episodes of anxiety, but my urge to binge and purge had finally disappeared. By now, the phrase "eating disorder" had become as familiar and commonplace as "breast cancer" or "heart disease." Every week, it seemed, women who struggled with bulimia were coming out and admitting it in public—from movie stars and television personalities, to Princess Diana.

After my initial confessional phone call to my mother years earlier—when she had responded, "Well, whatever it is you're dealing with, *I* certainly had nothing to do with it"—I never mentioned the subject again.

Nor did she.

Good News, Bad News

THE DAY CAME when Tom and I decided to move out of the city and to the suburbs, where raising our family would be easier and less expensive. We moved to New Canaan, a leafy Connecticut suburb with rolling stone walls and good public schools.

Although I missed the city, I liked the way everything about our new town was geared toward raising children. And I was surprised how much I enjoyed being "on our own" again as a family. Katy and Brinck quickly made friends and thrived at their new elementary school. They relished the freedom of our woodsy backyard and riding their bikes up and down the block. Tom didn't mind his one-hour train commute to the city—he said it gave him time to catch up on his reading. We found a good church. And we all enjoyed the slower pace of life—the sound of wind in the trees, the cheerful call of black-capped chickadees, even the sight of deer hungrily nibbling at the rhododendron bushes.

In our new suburban setting, I was surprised to discover

that there were some ways in which my mother and I weren't so different after all. I enjoyed entertaining and—like my mother—found myself preparing for company by gliding around the house lighting flickering votives and fragrant sticks of vanilla incense. I also found that I especially savored the quiet time—when everything was perfect and undisturbed—just before the guests arrived. With my bigger kitchen, I found myself baking cakes and cookies and taking them to friends who were "down in the dumps." I still didn't like clothes shopping. But when my mother came out from the city to visit, we discovered that we both enjoyed hunting for antiques, especially speculating endlessly about the possible stories behind each cracked and dusty artifact ("If only that antique shaving mug could talk!"). My mother had a green thumb, and now I discovered I liked gardening too. When she came to visit, she would *ooh* and *aah* over my clay flowerpots of cascading petunias, lush begonias and pink geraniums. Especially the geraniums.

Distance was definitely good for our relationship. Distance allowed me the emotional space to more easily do what every adult child must ultimately do in coming to terms with one's parents: accept, appreciate and practice their legacy of good and helpful things—while at the same time letting go of those things that were not so good and not so helpful.

One midsummer afternoon I was watering the pot of geraniums by the back door when the phone rang. It was my mother. She had just returned from the eye doctor, she said. And not just any eye doctor, but someone called a "retina specialist."

The news was not good.

"He says I have the beginnings of macular degeneration." Her voice was shaky. "It's in both eyes, and he says it will only get worse with time. He says—he says there is no cure . . ."

I'd never heard my mother sound so worried.

Because of my grandfather's blindness, I was familiar with age-related macular degeneration, a medical condition predominantly found in elderly adults in which the center of the inner lining of the eye, known as the macula area of the retina, suffers thinning, atrophy and in some cases bleeding. My mother was seventy-eight years old and in good physical health. But now one of her worst fears had come to pass. Like her father, my mother had the early stages of the "wet" form of macular degeneration, which meant that her vision loss was due to abnormal blood vessel growth, causing blood and protein leakage beneath the macula area of the retina.

I knew that blindness caused by macular degeneration did not mean that my mother would lose her peripheral vision or her ability to see light. It was not the kind of blindness that would ever require her to use a white cane.

But over time it would eventually cause a devastating loss of her *central vision,* which meant there was a good chance that someday she would no longer be able to read, or play bridge, or drive a car or recognize faces. There was the strong likelihood that someday—like her father—she would, indeed, go blind . . .

"But for *now,* your eyes are okay, right?" I asked.

My mother heaved a shuddery sigh.

"And maybe they'll stay okay for a long time," I ventured.

Silence.

"And every day new medical discoveries are being made," I said, trying my best to sound upbeat. "Who knows? Maybe one day soon they'll come up with a cure."

"Maybe," she said.

But she didn't sound too hopeful.

"Try not to worry," I said, as I hung up the phone.

I RETURNED TO THE POT OF GERANIUMS, and watched as the cool crystal water splashed on the delicate shell-pink blossoms, and ran in rivulets down the fuzzy green stems into the black loamy dirt. I'd watered the geraniums so many times before, but it was as though I was seeing them for the first time.

No wonder they are Mom's favorite, I thought.

I picked up the empty watering can and headed back to the house.

She might be okay for now, I worried. *But what will Mom do when the day comes that she can no longer see? How will she manage?* And then, a thought so troubling that it took my breath away . . .

Who will take care of her?

THAT NIGHT I phoned my sister.

"So what do you think about Mom's eyes?" I asked.

"Well, for *now* they're all right," said Carolyn.

"Yes," I said.

"And maybe they'll stay that way for a long time," she ventured.

"Maybe," I sighed.

"And who knows? Maybe one day soon they'll come up with a cure," she said.

"That's exactly what I told Mom."

"Don't worry," said Carolyn. "Everything will be all right."

"You think?"

"Absolutely," she said.

I wished I could be so sure.

Boundaries

A FEW WEEKS LATER, Tom and I got to talking about my mother's future. Lingering at the kitchen table after dinner, we talked about her vision problem and her fear of someday winding up in a nursing home. We talked about how her moving out of the city might be a good idea. Maybe to New Canaan. Maybe . . . into the empty in-law apartment attached to our house. Up until now we had used the extra space as a guest room. It was where my mother already stayed when she came to visit.

"I don't know if it's such a good idea," I initially said, my mind racing with a million reasons why.

We got along better at a distance. We were still so different in so many ways. She was so disorganized and spontaneous. I was a control freak. She liked to entertain friends at the drop of a hat, and loved it when people stopped by unexpectedly for tea and a chat. I liked having company too, but I preferred advance notice. Twenty-four hours. Minimum. And our relationship was *limited* by so many psychological barriers—each one, when accidentally stumbled upon, waiting to zap me like the invisible electric fence our neighbors had for their dog . . .

I felt like I couldn't breathe.

Oh, God. What would it be like having her right here with me? Every day? With nothing but a thin wall separating the two of us?

"It helps a lot," Tom calmly pointed out, "that the apartment has its own kitchen, its own bathroom and its own front and back doors."

"Yes," I agreed. "It even has its own miniwasher/dryer."

"And your mother would have her own mailbox and phone number," said Tom.

"Her own car too," I added.

"Plus, over the long term, it would be good for her financially," said Tom.

This was certainly true. Over the years the monthly maintenance fee on my mother's co-op apartment in the city had crept as high as some rents, and it would only go higher.

The more Tom and I talked it over, the better the idea sounded.

THE NEXT WEEKEND when my mother came out to visit, we asked her what she thought about the idea of moving in next door. For a long moment she was quiet. Then she said she liked the idea. She said it was practical. She said it made sense.

Yes, I told myself, *it does make sense.*

Now that my mother was getting older, I wouldn't worry so much about her if she was close by. We could get right to her if there was some emergency. Carolyn thought that it was a good idea too. And the kids were thrilled. The idea of having Mama B. living right next door, 24/7—her fridge covered with their artwork and photos, and filled with sweet treats—was like a dream come true.

Thankfully, my mother could still see well enough to read, keep up with her correspondence and play bridge. Most importantly, she could still see well enough to *drive*. With her perky champagne-colored Ford Escort, she would be able to visit friends, shop and do errands. She would be able to continue to be independent.

So we all agreed. She would move into the apartment.

STILL, I WORRIED. There was that distance between us. That yawning unbridgeable gap . . .

That night, I tossed and turned, unable to sleep.

"What are you worrying about now?" Tom reached over and turned on the light.

"Boundaries," I grumbled. "If we're going to go ahead with this, I feel it's important that Mom and I keep our households separate. I don't think we need to share *every* meal together. We won't necessarily need to see each other *every* day. I mean, some days we can just check in with each other by phone. Maybe it will help if I think of her apartment as not being actually attached to our house—but more like it's next door—or even down the street . . ."

"Kitty." Tom sat up on his elbows and regarded me sternly. "Did you ever stop to think that perhaps this move might not be so easy for your mother? For the past ten years, she's managed on her own in New York City. With the exception of her vision, her health is good. And you know how independent she is. She never asks for help."

You're right about that, I thought. If anything, that was probably the biggest difference between us. I was so weak, flawed and broken. I always seemed to need *so much* help. But not Mom.

"Take it easy," Tom said. "We've all given the situation a lot of thought. The decision has been made. Now have a little faith."

"You're right," I said, punching my pillow. "Good night."

Dear God, I prayed as I drifted off to sleep, *please help me.*

Unhappy Birthday

F ROM THE VERY START, my mother made it clear that she
intended to be as independent as possible. With her
car, she was able to come and go as she pleased. Optimistic
and outgoing, she quickly developed her own circle of
friends. Through my kitchen window, I marveled at the
parade of elegant gray-haired ladies who regularly arrived
at her back door for lively bridge parties, luncheons and
afternoon teas. Sometimes I could hear their laughter
through the kitchen wall. Things were going surprisingly
well. Until . . .

ON MY MOTHER'S EIGHTIETH BIRTHDAY, I pushed two
plump white candles shaped like the numbers 8 and 0 into
the chocolate frosting on her cake. I figured eight decades
was a milestone worth celebrating. But age, you may recall,
was something my mother preferred not to acknowledge.
"You are as old as you think you are," she liked to say. "And
I am thirty-nine and holding."

I lit the candles and carried the cake to the table. At

first my mother smiled with delight, but when I set the cake in front of her she frowned.

"What's that?" she asked.

"What's what?" I asked back.

"Those *candles*," she said.

"They're for your birthday," I replied. "*Eighty* years!"

The furrow between her eyebrows deepened. With a sinking feeling I realized my mistake.

"Oh, c'mon, Mom," I said, holding up my camera to take a photo. "Eighty years is something to celebrate. Now make a wish. And smile!"

"C'mon, Mama B!" Katy and Brinck echoed. "Smile!"

Reluctantly, she complied. The camera flashed, and the awkward moment was buried in cries of "Happy Birthday!" and "Hooray! Let's eat!"

A FEW MONTHS LATER, my mother complained of feeling faint. We went to the doctor, who told her that she had high blood pressure.

"That's impossible," she said. "High blood pressure is something fat people get. I'm not fat. I don't smoke. I eat well, and I take good care of myself."

"Well, Mrs. Brinckerhoff," the doctor said, "it is good that you take care of yourself. But sometimes, especially with age, a person can still have high blood pressure. Watch your salt intake," he said, scribbling a prescription. "And I want to see you again in two weeks."

On the drive home, my mother was uncharacteristically quiet. When suddenly she exploded with anger.

"It all started when you put those candles on that cake!" she blurted. "Until then, I was perfectly fine!"

"*What?*" I screeched, nearly going off the road. "Are you saying your high blood pressure is *my* fault? I cannot let you get away with that. *I* am *not* responsible for *your* health—or your happiness!" *There*, I thought. *I showed her . . .*

So why, I wondered as we drove toward home in icy silence, *do I feel so bad?*

We were pulling in the driveway when suddenly I understood why my mother had lashed out at me. She was afraid. This was her first major health problem. And deep down we both knew—despite her belief that age was all in the mind—that it likely wouldn't be the last.

"I'm sorry," I said.

"Me too," she replied.

"You're gonna be fine," I said. "It's just high blood pressure."

"I hope so," she said.

What I didn't tell my mother was that there was a part of me that was afraid too. Until now, I think I had always believed that she would live forever.

Heart of Stone

M Y MOTHER'S EYESIGHT was deteriorating, but I didn't know how bad it had gotten until the morning I saw her stooped in her living room, reaching to pick something off the floor. She grabbed at it and then studied her empty thumb and forefinger with a puzzled expression. Again she tried to pinch the glimmering spot on her living room rug. Nothing. Frowning, she turned to me. Behind the thick lens of her glasses, her blue-green eyes clouded with concern.

"Mom," I said, "it's just a patch of sunlight."

She shook her head, wary to admit something was wrong.

"We need to talk," she said.

IT WAS HARD TO BELIEVE that my mother had been living in the apartment attached to our house for nearly eight years. A widow for more than two decades, she was eighty-six years old.

Where had the time gone?

Over the years we had found ways to help with her macular degeneration. Tom installed bright halogen lights in her living room. My sister sent away for a special telephone with big print numbers. We used colorful plastic adhesive buttons to identify the proper settings on her thermostat, microwave and washer/dryer. We bought a high-tech electronic magnifying monitor to help her read her mail.

Despite her low vision, my mother had been able to maintain her independence, and so had I. She could still drive. She could still spend the whole afternoon shopping at the nearby Lord & Taylor department store if she wanted . . .

"WE NEED TO TALK," she repeated. "About my eyes."

"Oh, Mom," I said. "Don't worry about it."

"No," she said. "My vision has really gotten bad. I—I don't think I should be driving anymore." Her eyes filled with tears.

"It's okay," I said. "Don't worry. We'll work it out."

But I *was* worried. I should have been prepared for this day, but I wasn't. I thought things could stay as they were. I thought my mother would be able to drive forever. But she was going blind. And there was nothing we could do to stop it.

My head buzzed with worrisome questions.

If Mom no longer drives, who is going to take her to the grocery store? To doctors' appointments? To the hair salon? To the dry cleaners? To visit her friends? She was going to need help. Lots of it. My life was already so busy with two teenagers, work, a new puppy, and managing my own household.

How was I ever going to meet my mother's needs?

THE NEXT DAY, when I stopped by my mother's apartment to return her dry cleaning, I watched apprehensively as she opened her refrigerator door, peered inside and ran her hand over the contents on the top shelf.

"*Hmmm,*" she frowned. "I'm out of milk. And low on cottage cheese." She looked up at me hopefully. "Is there any chance you're going to the store today?"

"Maybe," I replied flatly. "Yeah. I guess."

"Thank you, Kitty," she said. "I really appreciate it." She closed the refrigerator door. "Oh, and one last thing," she said. "I've got a hair appointment scheduled for tomorrow morning. Is there any chance you could drop me off?"

"I'll have to check my calendar," I said, moving toward the door, eager to get out of her apartment before she remembered anything else. She was beginning to remind me of the old TV detective Columbo.

Closing the door behind me, I felt overwhelmed. Anxiety gripped my chest. The healthy boundaries I had worked so hard to build in order to peacefully coexist with my mother were suddenly becoming as blurred as her vision.

A FEW WEEKS LATER, while driving my mother home from a doctor's appointment, feelings of burden and resentment filled my head with a dull roar. We had just learned that in addition to her macular degeneration and high blood pressure, she was also suffering from some sort of heart problem.

She sat next to me in the front passenger seat of our minivan.

"So did you hear the latest about Vivian's two grand-children?" she asked.

Vivian was my mother's best friend.

"One got accepted to Yale, and the other's going to Harvard Law," she said.

Fixing my eyes on the road ahead, I said nothing.

"Viv is so proud of them," she went on. "They must be very good students . . ."

By now, I wasn't even listening. I was too busy think-ing instead about how the doctor had said that my mother needed to see a heart specialist, which meant *another* doc-tor's appointment, *another* afternoon lost.

I don't have time for this! I thought angrily.

"Kitty?" my mother asked.

"*What?*" I snapped.

Sensing my foul mood, she fell silent.

Great, I thought. *Now I've gone and hurt her feelings. Now I can add guilt to my long list of crummy feelings.*

WITH EACH PASSING DAY, feelings of burden, resentment and guilt (for feeling burdened and resentful) piled up like dirty laundry. It didn't help when some well-meaning friend would inevitably say, "Oh, Kitty, you're such a *good* daughter to be taking such good care of your mother." *No, I'm not,* I wanted to say. *Goodness has nothing to do with it. I'm a terrible daughter. Everything I do is more about duty than love. And there are days when I feel absolutely trapped.*

Worse was when someone would say, "Oh, Kitty, you're so *fortunate.* How I wish my mother was still *alive.* She was my *best friend* and I miss her *so* much!" *Your mother was your* best *friend?* I thought. *Well mine wasn't and isn't.* I felt a stab of jealousy. And then, of course, I felt more guilt—guilt for not feeling more grateful for *having* a mother, plus guilt for feeling jealous that she wasn't my best friend.

Every once in a while some refreshingly honest soul would blurt, "Oh, God, Kitty. I don't know how you do it. I could *never* live so close to my mother. It would drive me *crazy.*" *Yes!* I wanted to cry. *Thank you for understanding!* But all I said was, "Well, it's not always easy."

LATER, WHILE WALKING WITH TOM along a wooded path in a local park, I glanced down to see a perfectly heart-shaped pebble peeking out from a pile of old leaves. I stopped and picked it up. It was rough, cold and hard. A heart of stone.

Just like my heart, I thought.

I tucked the pebble in my jeans pocket, and we continued on our walk. When I got home, I set the pebble on the kitchen counter, next to the sink, where I could see it every day.

Dear God, I prayed, *soften my cold, hard heart.*

The Dream

A FEW NIGHTS LATER, I had a dream. In the dream, my mother was very frail and old, and concerned about the sudden appearance of a hump on her back.

"Look," she said, bending over to show me. "Can you see it?"

"Yes," I said. "I can see it." Her back was pale and bony. I shuddered with revulsion.

"Would you—touch it?" Her voice was anxious. Afraid.

Reluctantly I extended my hand—and the moment my fingers touched the hump, I was suddenly overcome with a wave of sorrow and compassion for my mother unlike anything I'd ever felt before.

Oh, Mom! I thought. *How terrifying it must be to grow old and have your body betray you. To know that you have absolutely no control over the future. To know that even though you're surrounded by family, death is something you must ultimately face on your own. How frightened you must be! Oh, Mom, I am so sorry!*

I woke up sobbing, unable to shake the dream's vivid, heart-wrenching emotion. It was all so strange. The compassion that I experienced in the dream was something I did not feel for my mother in real life. But in the dream it was so *real*. I wanted so badly to hold on to it and carry it with me into the waking daylight.

Is it possible, I wondered, *that the dream is God's way of showing me that someday I will be capable of feeling true compassion for my mother—even though I don't feel it now?*

But as the day wore on, I knew that if I was honest, there was a part of me that didn't want to feel compassion for my mother. There was a part of me that wanted to hang on to my anger and my unforgiving heart. It felt too good to let go. After all, my sense of burden and resentment was justified . . . Wasn't it?

Oh, it was all so confusing. Part of me wanted so desperately to let go and forgive the hurts of the past. But other parts of me . . . the anxious little girl . . . the angry teenager . . . the burdened, resentful adult . . . just wanted to fold my arms, shake my head, and stubbornly say, "*No! I can never forgive you. Not now. Not ever.*" There was something so *empowering* in not forgiving.

That night, before going to sleep, I opened my Bible to look for guidance, which only left me more confused and racked with guilt. Especially that particularly onerous Fifth Commandment: "Honor your father and your mother."

"What exactly does *that* mean?" I grumbled to Tom. "To *honor* your mother? I mean, what exactly does God want from me? Is there such a thing as giving up *too* much of one's life for another? Sometimes I feel like there's just not enough of me to go around."

"I don't know," said Tom. "Maybe you should talk to someone. You're not the only person dealing with an aging parent. Maybe there's someone who can help you."

NEXT DAY, I MADE AN APPOINTMENT to visit with one of the ministers at our church. She was an expert in geriatric pastoral concerns, beloved by many older members of the congregation for her open door and listening ear. Now she leaned forward and listened intently as I poured out my story—well, not the *whole* story. But the part about feeling overwhelmed about meeting my mother's ever-increasing needs.

"Oh, Kitty," she said. "It's so good you came to talk. You're a classic example of a woman trapped in the Sandwich Generation."

I'd heard of the Lost Generation. The Greatest Generation. The Pepsi Generation. The Me Generation. Generation X. But the *Sandwich* Generation?

"What's that?" I asked.

"You're being squeezed by responsibilities on both generational ends," she said. "You're caught between being a wife and mother, and taking care of your own mother. I imagine sometimes you must feel pretty squished." She smiled sympathetically.

"Yes!" I agreed. "There are days when that's exactly how I feel."

"You ask about the Fifth Commandment and what it means to 'honor' your mother," she said. "It's a good question. The word honor means to respect, to hold in high esteem. It can also imply a certain formality—even distance.

"You don't need to be best friends. Sometimes that's just not possible. God understands that you have primary responsibilities to your husband and children. He understands that you can't be all things to all people all the time—and I don't think He expects you to be."

She walked over to a tall file cabinet, opened the top drawer and pulled out a thick manila folder.

"It's important you realize that you're not alone," she said. "As people live longer, more and more of us find ourselves caring for aging parents. The good news is that there are many resources available to help you and your mom." She wrapped her arm around me. "You know, God put us here on earth to help each other."

With her help, I learned that our town provided a free service called the GetAbout Van for seniors who needed transportation. And two mornings a week, a company called Home Instead dispatched a cheerful, energetic woman named Debbie to help my mother with her correspondence, sorting photos, odd jobs and errands. Carolyn pitched in with frequent visits, and took my mother shopping and to her appointments in the city with a doctor who practiced "integrated medicine," and gave her special vitamins for her eyes. And all those friends whose laughter I heard through the wall—they were only too glad to help too.

Although my mother could no longer drive, life took on a sense of new normal. Soon I could hear her teakettle singing again on the other side of the wall.

ONE AFTERNOON, after tea with her friends, she came to me, giggling. "The girls had me sit on the floor because they said they wanted to watch me get up on my own. They couldn't believe I was so limber!"

I could hear the note of pride in her voice. Would I have ever gotten down on the floor in front of all my friends just to prove a point?

She sat down at the kitchen table and laughed her pretty, tinkly ice-cube laugh. Then she crossed her slender legs, arched one foot and twirled it languidly. For a moment I could almost see her Egyptian barefoot sandals that she had worn when I was growing up. I had to hand it to her. In her way, she was still sexy. She was still, as my father used to say, "the hostess with the mostest."

My mother had always been very proud of her personal appearance. Now she frequently asked me to put on her eyebrows with a brown eyebrow pencil, as she could no longer see to do it herself.

"You know," she said one day, as I sketched her eyebrows, "losing your eyesight isn't so bad. When you can't see the wrinkles, everyone looks beautiful!"

ONE OF THE MOST FRUSTRATING ASPECTS of low vision, was the way it was often misinterpreted by others as feeblemindedness. My mother had always been so proud of her Palmer Method penmanship—with its elegant loops and curls, a graceful extension of herself on the page. But now her handwriting was shaky and hard to read. Now words and sentences might be written one atop the other, or separated by large gaps. My mother's deteriorated handwriting was often misunderstood as being the result of being physically impaired. But she was not feeble, physically or mentally. She just couldn't see.

Likewise, when she used her typewriter, if she started with her hands in the wrong position—only one letter off—her sentences were reduced to nonsensical jibberish. For example, "Hello!" became "Jr;;pp@." Most of her long-distance friends understood this, and had fun "decoding" her typewritten letters. But for some, this was judged as a sign of her being confused. Again, it was simply the result of not being able to see.

Probably the most challenging aspect of macular

degeneration was that it stole my mother's central vision, making it difficult to recognize faces, even at close range. Many times people wrongly assumed that she was forgetful, when her mind was sharp as a tack. So sharp, in fact, that she became the cofounder of our town's Macular Degeneration Support Group.

DESPITE HER FAILING VISION and difficulty writing, my mother continued to correspond with relatives and friends from all around the country. One day, when I was reading my mother's mail out loud to her, I noticed a recurring theme in the letters: *"Dear Bess,"* they would all begin. *"I was feeling so low. But then I received your good letter. I don't know how you do it. Thanks for cheering me up!"*

Typically, after reading my mother's mail out loud to her, I could hardly wait to jump off the sofa and hurry back to my own house. But this day was different.

"Anything else you want me to read?" I asked.

"I don't think so," she shook her head.

"Okay, then," I stood to leave.

But my feet didn't want to move. I read somewhere once that courage was not about being fearless, but about taking action and moving forward *despite* being afraid. It occurred to me that my mother, in the positive way she dealt with her blindness, was probably the most courageous person I had ever known.

"Hey, Mom," I blurted impulsively, "I was just thinking—wouldn't it be fun to go to Lord & Taylor tomorrow for lunch and a little shopping? I hear they've got a big sale going on."

Her eyes lit up. "Do you mean it?" she asked. "You're so busy with work and the kids. Do you think you have the time?"

I nodded, and we wrapped our arms around each other. I was surprised by how tiny she had become. I towered over her and she seemed so small, so—vulnerable.

"Don't forget your fifteen percent-off coupon!" Mom called as we said good-bye. "If you don't have one, you can use mine."

"Thanks," I said.

When I returned to the kitchen, I picked up the heart-shaped pebble and turned it around in my hand. It was cold and hard and rough around the edges.

The way my heart used to be.

Table for Two

THE NEXT MORNING at Lord & Taylor, my mother and I split up to shop, agreeing to meet at noon at the department store's Signature Café. Although she could no longer drive, she was still able to see well enough to navigate the store's familiar aisles and escalators on her own. Many of the clerks knew her by name.

After dawdling over the lipsticks at the cosmetics counter, I took the escalator up to the second floor and killed some more time admiring the china and crystal giftware and purchasing a few greeting cards. After all these years, I was still not much of a shopper.

At noon, the café hostess led me to a table for two. As I waited for my mother, I fiddled with the artificial longstemmed red rose in a white plastic bud vase at the center of the table. I glanced at my watch and straightened the salt and pepper shakers. I organized the ceramic container of pink, blue and yellow packets of artificial sweeteners.

How much longer was she going to be? I thought impatiently.

I craned my neck and scanned the dining room, until across the room I saw her red hair. Her arms were laden with shopping bags, and she was chatting with the hostess.

"Mom!" I stood and waved, and then got up to take her bags and walk her to the table.

"So how'd you make out?" I asked.

"Oh, Kitty," she said, plopping onto her chair. "I had such *luck*!"

She dug into her shopping bags and pulled out a russet and amber paisley silk scarf and ivory long-sleeved, high-necked ruffled blouse. Both items, she said, were on sale. A *steal*. Plus, she'd been able to use her fifteen percent-off coupon. She was short of breath—which worried me a little bit. But she was happy.

I showed her my lipstick and greeting cards. And then I opened the menu and read the selections out loud to her. She would have a grilled cheese sandwich with tomato, she said, plus a side order of the café's "Signature Bread" and chocolate ice cream for dessert. As usual, she was trying to gain weight. I, on the other hand, would have the house salad, hold the croutons, dressing on the side and no dessert.

Some things never change, I thought.

As we waited for our food to arrive, there was an awkward silence. For a moment I felt as though I was back in high school, at a loss for something to say. Then my mother adjusted her glasses and cleared her throat.

"Kitty," she said. "There's something I've wanted to talk to you about for a long time."

Uh-oh, I thought. At least I no longer bit my fingernails.

It turned out she wanted to talk about her first marriage.

She told me that the reason why I'd stumbled across my sister's birth certificate so many years ago was because she and my father were in the midst of finalizing Carolyn's adoption. It was a process, she said, which had taken much longer than they had ever expected because every time they moved to a new state—which they did frequently in the early years of my father's career—they had to begin the paperwork all over again.

She went on. She met her first husband in college, she said. He was from a good family and very handsome, attentive and charming. He was smart and good and kind, she said. Until he drank. Then he became uncontrollably angry and irrationally jealous. Two times he went away for six weeks to take "the cure," which is what they called rehab back then, and both times she said she hoped and prayed that he would be healed of his alcoholism. But that isn't what happened. One terrible night he came home drunk, brandishing a gun and threatening to kill her— and their baby daughter. That's when she knew she had to leave him.

Family and friends were led to believe that she had moved with Carolyn from Niagara Falls to Reno, Nevada, to establish residency and get a divorce. But secretly—for fear of being followed by her enraged husband—she took a train to Miami, Florida, where her parents knew someone who owned an apartment building where she could live and take care of her baby while working as the building manager, renting out apartments. Because it was wartime, she said, times were tough. But she stayed in Florida until her residency was established and the divorce was final. It was during this time that she remet her old childhood friend—my father—and fell in love.

Even though her first marriage was a mistake, she said, she would do it all over again because without that marriage she would never have had Carolyn.

She wanted me to know what a wonderful husband and father Dad was (which, of course, I knew already), and how much he loved Carolyn from the moment he set eyes on her. She kept on talking, but suddenly I wasn't listening . . .

Instead I was dumbstruck with a new realization of what an incredibly *good mother* she had been to my sister. By choosing not to remain in an abusive, dangerous relationship, my mother had not only saved her own life—but the life of her daughter too. How brave she had been to get on that train with her baby, in the midst of wartime, and travel all the way to Florida! How strong! And again—such a *good mother*. What better, more gratifying and worthy legacy could any woman claim than to have *saved her child's life?*

"Mom," I said, "What you did took so much *courage.* Do you have any idea how good a mother you were?"

She shook her head. Her lower lip trembled and her eyes glinted with tears.

Inexplicably, I felt a swelling in my heart, as though it was physically expanding. And I felt the great yawning gap between my mother and me shrink just the tiniest bit.

In the car on the way home we were both quiet. But it wasn't the icy, awkward silence that we had endured so many times before.

It was a comfortable silence.

A silence that was somehow—peaceful.

LATER THAT EVENING, I phoned my sister and told her about our lunch.

"I still can't believe how brave Mom was," I said. "And such a good mother."

"Really?" asked Carolyn. "I've always thought of her that way. She may seem fluffy on the outside, but deep down inside she's strong. A real survivor."

"Yes," I agreed. "That, she is."

The Dancing Lesson

OVER THE YEARS, my mother had grown very fond of Tom. She said that he was a good man, and that I was lucky to have "found him."

"Well, we sort of found *each other*," I corrected her. It was a small thing, but I couldn't let it go. *Why am I always so eager to pick a fight?* I thought. My prickly churlishness was like a bad habit.

"You know, Kitty," she went on, ignoring my remark, "it may not always seem like it, but these are the best years of your lives. You two kids should do everything you can to make the most of them."

"Uh-huh," I replied, only half-listening. *Why does she insist on calling us "kids"?* And this wasn't the first time she had told me that these were "the best years of our lives." *Why does she keep on repeating the same thing over and over? As far as I can see, each year of married life is pretty much like all the others . . .*

THEN THE DAY CAME when our kids went off to college. They hadn't been gone more than a week when Tom surprised me

by saying how he thought it might be fun for the two of us—
after so many years—to finally learn how to dance.

Unlike my parents, dancing had never played a significant role in our relationship. Sure, we could do a primitive
slow dance, and we could hold our own in a stand-apart
fast dance. But we didn't know how to twirl to a waltz,
swivel our hips to a Latin beat or spin and swing to the jitterbug. Okay. I'll admit it. After nearly twenty-five years of
marriage, we still didn't know how to *dance*. At weddings
and dinner dances, it wasn't much fun to be left sitting at
the table when everyone else was up on the dance floor.

So I agreed. We would take dancing lessons.

When I told my mother, her eyes lit up.

"Dancing lessons!" she cried. "What a *wonderful* idea!
You two kids are going to *love* dancing."

"Aw, Mom," I said, "I don't know. We're not like you
and Dad."

I remembered my parents gliding across the kitchen
floor to the sweet strains of Benny Goodman and Peter
Duchin, finishing with a dramatic dip. My mother would
look up at my father with dreamy eyes and sigh, "Oh,
John." And he would respond in his best Ralph Cramden
voice, "Baby, you're the greatest!"

I also remembered how back in seventh grade, my
mother had signed me up for Sunday night cotillion
classes. I was shy, awkward and clumsy. I blamed it on the

boys. Their palms were sweaty. They stepped on my toes. Plus they were way too short. Our instructor was an elegant older gentleman with slicked-back pewter hair and a pencil moustache who tried his best to teach the box-step to the creaky beat of Jimmy Gilmer and the Fireballs' "Sugar Shack." All I wanted to do was tear off my short white gloves and race home in time to see the Beatles sing "I Wanna Hold Your Hand" on *The Ed Sullivan Show*.

AT OUR FIRST DANCING LESSON, I placed my left hand on Tom's shoulder, and extended my right arm. He, in turn, rested his right hand on the small of my back, and placed his left hand in mine. So far, so good . . .

When suddenly, inexplicably, I felt as though I was back in seventh grade—shy and insecure about being so close to this strange boy. My heart pounded and my palms were sweaty. *If only I had my little white gloves!*

Our instructor was an upbeat middle-aged man named Charlie, who wore a pale blue golf shirt, navy blazer and comfortable leather loafers. Light as a feather, he moved smoothly alongside us demonstrating a supposedly simple waltz step. But for some reason I found it impossible to listen to Charlie's instructions and the music, while moving. When he opened his mouth, his voice sounded like the muted trumpet *"wah-wah-wah"* of the teacher in the animated *Peanuts* cartoons. No matter how hard I tried to concentrate, I was unable to make my feet do what they were supposed to do.

"Left-two-three. Right-two-three . . ." Charlie chanted.

But whose left? Whose right? Tom's or mine?

"Back-two-three. Forward-two-three . . ."

Stiff and awkward, I felt like an idiot. Plus, I was getting hot. I stuck out my lower lip and blew a blast of cool air under my bangs. This dancing was hard work. Why, it was practically a *sport!*

At the end of the class, Charlie handed Tom a CD that included a mix of music for slow dancing, the cha-cha-cha, the waltz and the jitterbug. "See you next week," he said as he waved good bye. "And remember to practice!"

In the car on the way home, I took off my shoes and massaged my aching toes.

"So what do you think?" I asked Tom.

"I think you need to get yourself a more comfortable pair of shoes," he suggested.

After dinner, he pushed aside the glass-topped coffee table and overstuffed chair in the sunroom to create a space for dancing. It wasn't a very large space, but the floor was hardwood, and it was where the CD player was located. For the next two nights we practiced. First the slow dance, then the cha-cha-cha, the waltz and the jitterbug.

With every dance, I thought I kept the beat better than

Tom. And I told him so. Which, upon seeing his slightly hurt expression, I immediately regretted.

So, which is more important? I wondered, as we lurched past the sofa and potted plants. *Keeping the beat, or following Tom's lead? I don't like following. And why should I follow anyway? Tom doesn't know any more about dancing than I do.*

And then, on our third night practicing, a strange thing happened.

For a moment, I forgot about keeping the beat, or watching my feet, or paying attention to whether I was leading or following. I simply closed my eyes and relaxed. It was just the two of us, lost in the music . . .

Dancing.

"Hey," Tom whispered. "You're good."

"No," I said. "It's you."

I remembered how I had felt when we first met—the strong attraction, the blissful lightheadedness. It was all so . . . *romantic.*

No wonder my parents enjoyed dancing so much, I thought.

THE NEXT MORNING I bumped into my mother outside her back door where she was waiting for a friend to pick her up to go to the Ladies' Guild meeting at church. While her low vision prevented her from working on the group's fund-raising crafts projects, the women insisted that she come to the meetings anyway. They said they enjoyed her company. They also enjoyed her plates of fresh-baked homemade chocolate cake and banana bread.

"So how are the dancing lessons going?" she asked.

"So far, so good," I said.

"Glad to hear it. Are you practicing?"

I nodded. "Every night. In the sunroom."

"Good," she said. "It's the practicing that makes all the difference."

"That's exactly what our instructor told us," I said.

"Sounds like you have a good teacher."

She smiled, and her eyes got a faraway look. I knew what was coming next.

"Remember, Kitty," she said, "it may not always seem like it, but these are the best years of your lives. You two kids should do everything you can to make the most of them."

For some reason this time it didn't bother me so much that she called us "kids." And it didn't matter that she had told me that these were "the best years of our lives" more times than I could remember.

A car horn sounded from the driveway.

"There's my ride," she said.

I watched as she made her way down the back steps. Slender and erect, she wore a fashionable leopard-print silk scarf draped around her neck, and a wide black belt cinched her narrow waist. Her auburn hair was coiffed in the same short fluffy teased 'do she had worn back when I was in high school. As she descended the concrete stairs, she gripped the white wooden railing tightly and her lips moved slightly as she counted each step . . . "eight . . . nine . . . ten . . ." until she safely stepped onto the driveway. Before getting into her friend's car, she turned and waved.

I knew she couldn't see me, but I waved back anyhow.

A bittersweet pang tugged at my heart as I suddenly grasped the hard-earned wisdom of what my mother—a woman acquainted with loss—had been trying for so long to tell me: *Tom and I would not have each other forever.* Soon enough, the day would come when one of us would be gone. If only for the simple fact that we were together, each day was a gift to be appreciated . . . savored . . . lived to the fullest. With or without dancing . . .

My mother was right.

These *were* the best years of our lives.

Time

A FEW WEEKS BEFORE CHRISTMAS, my mother complained of shortness of breath. Her legs hurt and her usually thin ankles were swollen. Her blood pressure was high too. The cardiologist sent her to get an echocardiogram. In the examination room I guided her thin arms through the gaping holes of a huge blue paper gown. How tiny and frail she looked.

When had she gotten so old? I wondered.

The news was not good. My mother had congestive heart failure caused by age-related stenosis, or calcification of her aortic valve. Because of her advanced age and high blood pressure, she was not a good candidate for heart valve replacement surgery.

"But with the proper medication," the cardiologist said to me privately, "she should be able to live another two or three years."

Two or three years, I thought in dismay. *That's so little time!*

THE DAY AFTER CHRISTMAS, Tom, Mom, Carolyn, and I gathered around the breakfast table for a family meeting to discuss my mother's medical options. In the end, rather than take on the considerable risks associated with open-heart surgery, she decided to manage her congestive heart failure with medications.

In short order, we adjusted to another new "normal." Living with congestive heart failure meant more doctor visits—plus following a strict salt-free diet, and several new pills. Every day she had to be weighed to make sure that she wasn't retaining too much water. We sewed extra buttons on her pants' and skirts' waistbands to accommodate her swollen tummy. Sometimes it hurt for her to walk, so Carolyn bought her a pair of soft fleece-lined slippers for her puffy tender feet.

Ever the optimist, my mother chose not to focus on the cardiologist's gloomy prognosis, but talked instead about "getting better."

One afternoon while sorting a month's supply of her meds into four oversized plastic boxes labeled for the days of the week, my elbow accidentally bumped the top box and sent dozens of pills spilling onto the kitchen floor. Getting down on my hands and knees to retrieve them, I felt overwhelmed with sadness.

God, I prayed, *why does it have to end like this?*

Then, in my heart, I heard a familiar voice. Stern but tender: *I'm giving you this time with her.*

There was something reassuring and encouraging

about the message, and I repeated it over and over in my mind.

Is it possible, I wondered, *that as difficult and painful as these days might be, they are something not to run away from, but to embrace? That locked within them might be some hidden greater meaning and purpose?* But even if this was true, it didn't take away the pain and sorrow. It didn't make life one bit easier.

I gathered up the pills and set about the tedious task of resorting them and putting them back in the plastic containers.

I'm giving you this time with her.

One day I would understand.

But not yet.

Facing Fears

M Y MOTHER, you may recall, had two fears about growing old—that she would one day lose her vision, which, sadly, came to pass, and that she would one day wind up in a nursing home, which thankfully she did not.

I had a fear too.

Although I never breathed a word of it to anyone, I worried that one day my mother's physical infirmities would become so acute that she would need me to care for her in some impossibly intimate way. When it came to caregiving, I had my limits. *I am not a nurse*, I told myself. There were some things I just wouldn't—that I *couldn't*—do.

One day my mother said she felt achy and chilled, as though she was getting the flu. The next day she complained of an excruciating stabbing pain in her lower back and intestines. There was no throwing up or diarrhea. Just pain, she said. Then, the next day, she said the pain was worse.

"There's something terribly wrong," she said. Her eyes clouded with fear.

"Okay, Mom," I said, "let's take a look."

I tugged at her trousers and was horrified to see that her bottom—the left side of her bottom, to be exact—was covered in a mass of ugly blisters.

"Oh, Mom," I said. "It looks like you've got chicken-pox or something."

We rushed to the doctor who took one look and said, "I'm so sorry, Mrs. Brinckerhoff. You've got shingles. But I'll be darned if I've ever seen a case so nasty. And the location—" he shook his head. "I've never seen anything like it."

He went on to explain that shingles (technically known as *herpes zoster*) was a viral infection caused by the varicella-zoster virus, the same virus that causes chickenpox. After a person has had chickenpox, he said, the virus lies dormant in your nerves. Years later, the virus can reactivate as shingles. About one in ten healthy adults who've had chicken-pox eventually develops shingles, usually after age fifty. The shingles rash, he explained, always occurs on only *one side* of the body—most commonly appearing as a band of blisters that wraps from the middle of the back around one side of the chest to the breastbone, following the pathway of the nerves where the virus had lain dormant. Sometimes the blisters appear on one side of the neck or face, or around one eye. But to appear on one side of one's derriere—as they had on my mother—was, according to the doctor, most unusual.

The good news, he said, was that although painful, the typical shingles rash would likely heal after a week or two with no lasting effects.

But as weeks passed, it became clear that my mother's case was *not* typical. The blisters eventually healed and the skin looked normal, but the excruciating pain did *not* go away.

We returned to the doctor, who said that my mother had a most unfortunate complication of shingles called *postherpetic neuralgia.* Her nerve fibers had been permanently damaged in a way that caused her skin to be so sensitive that the slightest brush of clothing felt like an assault of fiery darts. The only relief to be found, the doctor said, was through a regular cleansing of the affected area with warm soap and water, followed by applications of a prescribed analgesic cream.

On the way home, we stopped at the pharmacy. My mother waited in the car while I ran in to pick up her prescription. As I stood in line at the counter, it occurred to me that because of her blindness, the care my mother needed was something that she could not do on her own.

She would need help.

No, I thought, *I am not a nurse. I cannot do this.*

Back home, I held my mother's arm as we slowly walked up the back stairs to her door. Every step, I could tell, was agony for her. And not just physically. Knowing that she had permanent nerve damage and would have to live with this excruciating pain for the rest of her life took a huge toll on her emotionally. My mother had always been a strong woman. A survivor. But now, for the first time in her life, it was as though her spirit was broken. For the first time in her life, she was profoundly *discouraged*.

By the time we reached the top step, she leaned against me, breathing heavily. Tears filled her eyes, and she shook her head helplessly.

"I don't know what I'm going to do," she said. "It hurts so bad."

"Oh, Mom," I said, "I'm so sorry." I fished in her pocketbook for her key. "Here," I said, and opened her door, "you sit down and catch your breath, and I'll be back in a minute."

I rummaged under my kitchen sink and found a pair of lavender latex gloves. Taking a deep breath, I pulled them on and returned to her apartment.

"Okay," I said, holding up my gloved hands like a surgeon about to scrub in, "Dr. Slattery will see you now."

She smiled weakly.

I opened the tube of analgesic ointment. "Now just relax," I said. "This might hurt a little bit at first, but it will make you feel much better." For a fleeting moment I remembered the countless times I'd cared for my children in physically intimate ways when they were babies. I never minded that. How was this so different?

At first my mother flinched, but as the cool creamy balm began to work she relaxed. And with each gentle stroke, a strange thing happened. With each stroke, it felt as though I was not only wiping on the soothing salve, but simultaneously wiping *away* the tears from long ago hurts . . . forgotten regrets . . . past misunderstandings . . .

When suddenly I was overcome with a wave of sorrow and compassion for my mother unlike anything I'd ever felt before.

Oh, Mom! I thought. *How terrifying it must be to grow old and to have your body betray you . . . How frightened you must be! Oh, Mom, I am so sorry . . .*

I remembered the dream when I had reluctantly extended my hand to touch the hump on my mother's back. But this wasn't a dream. The compassion I was feeling for my mother was *real*.

Beautifully, miraculously real.

WHY, I WONDERED LATER THAT EVENING, *had I worried so about taking care of my mother this way?* It was easy. Natural. As easy and natural as when I had cared for my children when they needed me.

I didn't need to be a nurse to care for my mother.

I only needed to be a daughter.

Happy Birthday

A FUNNY THING HAPPENED on my mother's ninetieth birthday.

Not wanting to make the same mistake I'd made ten years earlier, I did *not* decorate her cake with two plump candles in the shape of the numbers 9 and 0. I decorated it instead with fresh strawberries and a single slender white candle in the middle.

As I guided my mother down the back steps to the table set up in our small backyard, I was careful not to mention her age. But much to my surprise, *she* did.

"Can you believe I'm ninety?" she asked, as I settled her in her chair.

"No," I shook my head. "I can't."

Carolyn, who had come out from the city and was staying overnight, looked at me with raised eyebrows, as if to say, "*Oh my gosh. Did she* really *say that?*" I shrugged my shoulders and shot Katy and Brinck a warning glance that said, *Remember, don't talk age.*

"Okay, everybody!" I chirped, eager to change the

subject. "Time to sing 'Happy Birthday'!" I lit the cake's solitary candle and took a photo of my mother blowing it out.

Later, when the party was over and I carried my mother's bag of birthday gifts to her apartment, I overheard her talking on the phone.

"Oh, *thank you* for remembering my birthday!" she exclaimed. Her voice was lilting and happy, and she laughed her pretty ice-cube laugh. "I'm ninety years old today! Can you believe it?"

I set the bag of gifts by her back door and returned to the kitchen. Through the wall, I listened as her phone rang again . . . and again. I sliced a generous wedge of birthday cake, placed it on a paper plate, and covered it with plastic wrap. When I carried the slice of cake to her back door, I heard her voice, girlish and delighted.

"That's right," she was saying. "*Ninety!* Can you imagine?"

THE NEXT MORNING, there was a large piece of paper folded and scotch-taped to my kitchen door. I recognized my mother's handwriting, oversized and shaky, but elegant as ever. I opened the page and read:

That was my favorite party and I have had 90 birthdays and that one U gave me was the best one of all!

Thank U.

Mama B.

P.S. Phone rang all day.

My mother was no longer "thirty-nine and holding."

She was ninety years old.

And proud of it.

A Closer Bond

THROUGHOUT HER LIFE, my mother had been an early riser. But now the sound of her whistling teakettle, the noise of the television, the thump of her kitchen cabinet doors came later and later in the day. The friends still visited, but not in big groups anymore. And the laughter was quieter. There were no more shopping sprees, of course.

Each morning I peeked through the blinds of her back door and watched her tiny shoulders and chest rise and fall as she slept. *How strange*, I thought, *how our roles have become reversed, and how she is now like my child.* Grief tugged at my heart. How I feared the morning that I would find that she wasn't moving at all. Daily I braced myself for that moment, knowing it had to come. I told myself it would be a blessing if she could simply die peacefully in her sleep. Still, I dreaded it.

THEN, ON A SUNDAY MORNING in August, two months after her ninetieth birthday, my mother did not get out of bed. She was weak and hot and thirsty. I phoned the doctor, who said if she wasn't feeling better by noon, to call for an ambulance to take her to the hospital. Then I phoned Carolyn in New York, who said she would come right away.

In recent days, my mother had craved oranges, and kept a bag of them chilled in her refrigerator. Now I took one out and set it on her kitchen counter. I sliced it into eight segments, placed one on a paper napkin, and carried it into her bedroom.

"Mom?"

She opened her eyes.

"Does this look good to you?" I held the cool sweet fruit to her lips and watched as she ate it hungrily.

"More?"

She shook her head, and closed her eyes.

I returned to the kitchen and put the remaining orange slices in a glass Pyrex custard dish, and covered it tightly with plastic wrap.

Minutes later, Carolyn arrived and we called for the ambulance.

AT THE HOSPITAL, a wirelike temporary pacemaker was inserted through a port in my mother's shoulder to regulate her heartbeat. To keep her alive.

But the next day her organs were failing.

That night, our family gathered around my mother in

her hospital bed. Carolyn held one hand. I held the other. Tom stood at the foot of the bed. It wouldn't be long. Katy and Brinck murmured tearful words of love and hugged their grandmother good-bye. She nodded. She was still with us. Barely.

I looked down. Her lips moved ever so slightly. I bent my head closer.

"Help me," she whispered.

"We're here, Mom," I squeezed her hand tightly. Her breathing was so slow. I was certain that each breath would be her last. And then . . .

"Help me," she said again.

Help you? I looked to my sister and Tom. How could we help her? We'd done everything the doctors said we could. There was nothing more we could do. Then I understood. *My mother wasn't asking for help to live—but to die.* In the strangest way, I felt like a midwife at the bedside of a woman about to give birth—except my mother was laboring to move on to the next life.

"Help me."

Never had I heard two more heartbreakingly beautiful words.

Tears rolled down my cheeks. "We're with you, Mom. I love you. It's all right."

Her breathing grew shallow. Breaths came farther apart. I thought of my message from God.

I'm giving you this time with her . . .

I remembered how I had feared my mother moving in with us. Instead it had been an amazing gift. Even now, as her soul was leaving us, I felt something incredible. In the space between those final breaths, that distance I'd always felt between my mother and me evaporated.

For a brief moment the air in the room seemed to vibrate with the wings of a thousand angels.

And then there was no breath.

She was gone.

THAT NIGHT AS WE SAT around the kitchen table talking and reminiscing, I remembered how I had worried so about my mother's dying. In the end God, in His great love, had given me the unexpected gift of helping her to be born into her new eternal home in heaven.

Why, I wondered, *had I worried so?* God had known what He was doing all along. His timing and ways were not like mine.

Later that night, as I reached to turn off my bedside lamp, I thought again about how different I'd been from my mother. I remembered the lunch we shared at the Signature Café at Lord & Taylor, when I felt my heart physically expand and the gap between us miraculously began to shrink.

Now, as I drifted off to sleep, something unexpected

crept into my mind. Tomorrow I would go to her favorite store, and I would shop for just the right dress to wear for her funeral . . .

All afternoon, if necessary.

The Black Dress

T IME OF DEATH?"

The funeral director held his pen in the air, his eyebrows arched expectantly.

Such a simple question.

But no one answered.

"I've got it here somewhere." I fumbled in my bag for the hospital form the doctor on duty had given me the night before.

Tom, Carolyn and I were seated around a coffee table in the front parlor of New Canaan's Hoyt F. Funeral Home. The atmosphere was hushed and subdued. It was a sunny August afternoon, but the room was lit in a way that you couldn't tell whether it was day or night outside. My mother's body was in the next room. It had been her wish that her remains be interred alongside my father's in the columbarium at Arlington National Cemetery, in Virginia. We had come to the funeral home for one last good-bye.

"I can call the hospital if you can't remember the time

of death," the director said. "But I need it for the death certificate."

"No, no, I'm sure I've got it here somewhere."

I thought back to the night before in the hospital room, when my mother had died. But the *exact* time of death? Who could say? Yes, there had been a last breath. A final heartbeat. But after that? Her life had simply slipped away like water through a crack in time, finding its way to infinity's timeless ocean. It had all been so mysterious. Was it her soul that had left her body? Or her body that had left her soul? I remembered how I'd sensed angels being in the room with us, and the memory of it made me shiver. The veil between heaven and earth had been so thin as to be transparent. One thing I knew for certain: My mother had *not* died when the doctor, wearing a stethoscope around his neck and carrying a clipboard in his hand, had gently ushered us out of the room and closed the curtains around her bed. By then she had long departed this world. By then she not only had arrived in heaven—she had been there forever.

I pulled a flimsy yellow document out of my handbag, put on my reading glasses, and ran my finger down the lines of information . . .

Name: Elizabeth Johnson Brinckerhoff
Date of Birth: June 20, 1915
Place of Birth: Niagara Falls, New York
Cause of Death: Heart Failure . . .

"Time of Death: Ten thirty-five PM," I read.

"Thank you." The funeral director scribbled down the information, clicked his pen and stood up. "Would you like to view the body now?"

No! I thought. *Everything is happening too fast.* But I nodded and followed Carolyn and Tom into the viewing room.

Wrapped in a white sheet, my mother's body was lying on a flat slab—lifeless and uninhabited, like a dress that she had suddenly stepped out of and left behind in a rumpled pile. *Like the grave clothes in the tomb*, I thought.

Yes, her body was there. But the person who had been my mother was gone—irretrievably, absolutely gone. The sense of separation and loss was so acute as to be almost unbearable.

"Oh, Mommy, Mommy, Mommy," I cried. The words came from some deep, forgotten place in my soul. I couldn't remember ever having called my mother "Mommy." But suddenly I was so very young . . . six . . . four . . . two years old. Such a very little girl—utterly brokenhearted and lost without my mother.

I stroked her auburn curls, and gently pulled at them to frame her face. Just the way she liked. One last time.

"Good-bye," I whispered, kissing her cheek.

And then it was time to go.

BACK HOME, Carolyn and I entered the apartment where our mother had spent the last twelve years of her life. We were exhausted, but determined to pick up the place and prepare it for our out-of-town relatives who would be arriving later in the week for the funeral service.

I opened the refrigerator, and there in the glass Pyrex custard dish, covered with plastic wrap, were the orange segments I had prepared for my mother just forty-eight hours earlier. A lifetime ago.

I unwrapped the dish, and carried it to the bedroom where Carolyn and I leaned against Mom's dresser and closed our eyes as we enjoyed the cool, refreshing fruit. For a brief moment it was as though she was there with us—the three of us united in mystical communion as we shared what had been our mother's last taste of earth's sweet pleasures.

Standing there next to my sister, I remembered my disastrous first attempt at baking a cake when I was a child. What was it Carolyn had called it? Oh yes, the "bird cake." I remembered the purple finches swooping in from the woods to feast on the pile of broken crockery and cake crumbs. How patient my sister had been with me, that long-ago day. How loving. And although she couldn't know it then, she had planted the seeds of what would turn out to be an invaluable lesson: *In God's economy, nothing in life goes to waste. Something beautiful and good can come out of life's most difficult circumstances and mistakes.*

"I love you," I said to Carolyn.

"I love you too," she cried.

We hugged each other tightly and let the tears flow.

BY THE TIME CAROLYN PULLED OUT of the driveway to return to her apartment in the city, the summer sun hung low, a glowing crimson ball in a golden sky. I looked at the clock on the kitchen wall: *Eight o'clock!* I remembered the promise I'd made to myself the night before to find a dress for my mother's funeral. If I wanted to make the sale at Lord & Taylor, I was going to have to hurry!

As I rode the escalator up to the department store's second floor, I said a little prayer. *Please God, help me find the right dress.*

But after searching the racks of dresses, I came up with nothing.

Just my luck, I thought. Everything was either the wrong size or too short or too dressy or too expensive. For a fleeting moment I remembered shopping with my mother at Sears when I was little, and how she had tried to help me by suggesting that dark colors had a "slimming effect." My heart sank even deeper with discouragement.

I was about to leave when I took one last look at the clearance rack. And there, among a jumble of picked-over garments, was the perfect dress—black with a delicate lace bodice and cap sleeves. A bright orange sticker on the tag indicated that the dress had been marked down three times from its original steep price. But would it fit?

"Do you need any help?" The saleswoman asked, looking at her watch. "I don't mean to rush you, but we'll be closing soon."

"I'll just be a minute," I said, heading for the dressing room.

Amazingly, the dress fit perfectly.

At the check-out counter, I handed the saleswoman the dress.

"How pretty," she said, punching the buttons on the register. "And it's a bargain too. Seventy-five percent off from the last marked-down price."

"Great!" I said. "Oh, wait. I've got a coupon." I fished in my purse for a fifteen-percent-off coupon that my mother had given me just days earlier.

The saleswoman scanned the coupon, punched a few more buttons, and looked at the screen with wide eyes.

"Oh my," she said, and handed me the sales receipt.

I stared in disbelief at the amount: $7.99.

"If only my mother could see this," I said. "She always loved a good bargain. The dress is for her—funeral . . ."

And then I fell apart.

Stardust

ONE WEEK AFTER THE FUNERAL, the house was empty. Everyone had returned to their homes, back to their jobs, schools and busy lives. It was six-thirty in the evening. Tom would be home soon. I reached for the kitchen TV remote to turn on the evening news, and then changed my mind. Wrapped in a cocoon of grief, I was not yet ready for noise and chatter from the outside world.

Max, our roly-poly pug, followed me from the refrigerator to the sink as I prepared a salad for dinner—crisp romaine lettuce and cherry tomatoes, topped with sliced grilled chicken, and garnished with fresh blueberries. He made a snuffling sound, like a little pig searching for truffles—and looked up at me beseechingly with soulful brown eyes.

I deliberately allowed a blueberry to roll off the counter (Max had me well-trained), which sent him scurrying across the kitchen, his nails making a *clickety-clackety* sound on the wooden floor—a hound in hot pursuit. Well, not exactly a hound. Maybe more like an ewok. Max possessed an abundance of something zoologists actually call the "cute factor." With his large round head, flat face, floppy ears and big front-facing eyes, he ranked right up there in animal kingdom cuteness with pandas, koala bears and baby seals.

My mother had loved Max. She had called him her "granddog," and welcomed his frequent visits to her apartment, where she spoiled him with handfuls of granola and spoonfuls of vanilla ice cream. He, in turn, had delighted her with his repertoire of tricks, including "Roll over," "Bow," and "Dance." Or, as my mother preferred to say, "*Dancy-dancy!*" There was something about Max that inspired baby talk.

Now that my mother was gone, he had no interest in visiting her empty apartment.

As I watched our dog chase the blueberry, I glanced into the adjoining room and saw that I had forgotten to water the flowers on the dining room table. After my mother died, they had been the first flowers to arrive—a lush arrangement of stargazer lilies, irises and roses. Wrapped in crinkly cellophane and festooned with a pink satin bow, they were so beautiful that my first impulse had been to carry them next-door to show her.

Now the lilies had dropped their petals, the irises had wilted, and the heads on the cream and peach-colored roses drooped sadly.

Like me, I thought.

"HEY." IT WAS TOM, home from work. "How are you doing?"

"Okay, I guess." I wiped my hands on a kitchen towel.

"I've got something I think you might enjoy," he said. "Follow me." He took my hand and led me past the drooping flowers, into the sunroom.

"What is it?" I asked.

"Close your eyes," he said.

I listened to the familiar sound of the glass-topped coffee table and overstuffed chair being pushed aside, the click of a disc being placed in its slot, the whir of the CD player door closing. And then . . .

"Listen," Tom said. "It's a new recording of old standards by Rod Stewart. I thought you might like it. The title song is 'Stardust.'" He extended his hand and smiled.

"Shall we dance?"

I relaxed in Tom's arms, and as we danced, the sadness in my heart gradually lifted, like a morning mist kissed away by the warmth of the sun. For a moment I felt as though we were floating on a cloud.

Like Mom and Dad in heaven, I thought . . .

As the last note faded, we dipped and then slowly rose. Not as smooth and graceful as my parents, when as a child I watched them glide across the kitchen floor.

But for this evening, smooth enough.

That night, as I drifted off to sleep, the haunting melody of "Stardust" wove its way through my thoughts . . .

THE STORIES OF OUR LIVES, it occurred to me, are like songs —beautiful, eternal songs composed by a loving God. Here on earth, we cannot begin to comprehend the Author's intentions. "For now we see through a glass, darkly," the apostle Paul wrote, "but then, in heaven, face to face. For now on earth I know in part—but then, in heaven, I shall know fully—even as I am also fully known."

Even with our human limitations, there are moments on earth when heaven breaks through and we perceive with breathtaking clarity a completed stanza of our life's song. We are forgiven, and find that we can forgive. We are loved and find that we can love. We are saved . . . set free . . . healed . . . reconciled. When such amazing moments of grace occur, we marvel at their beauty and perfect rhyme. We can sense the Author's loving presence. We can hear His whisper in our hearts. Then, our spirits sing with deep meaning, purpose, faith and hope.

In heaven, God promises, we will see and hear everything clearly. In heaven, everything will finally make sense. The good and loving Author will take His children by the hand and show us how all the heartache, troubles, loss and tears of this life were just unfinished stanzas of our songs waiting to be completed—unfinished stanzas waiting to be rhymed with the miraculous ink of His redemptive grace.

In heaven, God will show us how nothing in life goes to waste. How *everything* in life has value—even the pain—and how something beautiful and good can rise from the rubble of life's most difficult circumstances and mistakes. From illness, He will show us His beautiful song of healing . . . from addiction, a song of deliverance . . . from a hardened heart, a song of compassion . . . from hurts and misunderstandings, a song of forgiveness . . . from estrangement, a song of reconciliation.

Indeed, it is entirely possible that in heaven I may look back at my years on earth—especially the hard times—and say, "Oh, why did I worry so? If only I'd known that my song was still being written, and that I was halfway to heaven all along."

I PULLED THE COMFORTER up under my chin.

"'Night, God," I murmured sleepily.

Good night, He replied. *Sweet dreams.*

How to Get Help

I F YOU OR SOMEONE YOU LOVE is struggling with an eating disorder, help is available. In recent years, significant advances have been made in the understanding and treatment of eating disorders. There is no longer any reason to suffer alone in silence. You can be healed.

First, it is essential that you *tell someone about your problem*. Your family physician is a good person to start with. Additional information and help is available at the following Web sites:

National Eating Disorders Association (NEDA)
www.nationaleatingdisorders.org

The Renfrew Center
www.renfrewcenter.com

Academy for Eating Disorders (AED)
www.aedweb.org

Wilkins Center
www.wilkinscenter.com